Unit C

StarBase Earth

The Solar System and Beyond

I WONDER

Wondering about the universe has led to the science of astronomy. What do you wonder about when you look at a starry sky?

Work with a partner to make a list of questions about the universe. Be ready to share your list with the rest of the class.

◄ Spiral Galaxy

▼ Jupiter

I PLAN

You may have asked questions such as these as you wondered about the universe. Scientists also ask questions. Then they plan ways to find answers to their questions. Now you and your classmates can plan how you will investigate the universe.

My Science Log

Why can't we see the stars during the day?

How far away is the sun?

How are the other planets like Earth?

How are the planets alike? How are they different from each other?

TOUR

With Your Class

Plan how your class will use some of the activities and readings in the **I Investigate** part of this unit. Decide what other resources you might use.

On Your Own

There are many ways to learn about the universe. Following are some things you can do to explore the universe by yourself or with some classmates. Some explorations may take longer to do than others. Look over the suggestions and choose . . .

- **Projects to Do**
- **Places to Visit**
- **Books to Read**

PROJECTS TO DO

STARBASE EARTH LOG

Be your own astronomer. Observe the sky on several nights and record your observations in a StarBase Earth Log. You might record the time the moon rises each night for a month. You could draw the moon's phases over that same period. Or you could keep a record of the brightest stars you can see. Set aside several pages in your StarBase Earth Log for each set of observations or drawings.

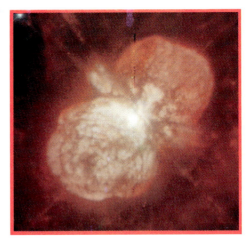

ASTRONOMY UPDATE

Collect information about new discoveries, recent satellite and space shuttle launches, or any other interesting space events. Check newspapers, magazines, radio and TV programs, and up-to-date books. Keep your information in a notebook, and present it in a report titled "Astronomy Update."

SCIENCE FAIR PROJECT

Review the **I Wonder** questions you and your partner asked. One way to find answers to these questions is through a science fair project. Choose one of your questions. Plan a project that would help you answer the question. Discuss your plan with your teacher. With his or her approval, begin work by collecting materials and resources. Then carry out your plan.

PLACES TO VISIT

BRING THE UNIVERSE INDOORS

An observatory or a planetarium is a wonderful place to learn about the universe. Ask your teacher to direct you to an observatory or a planetarium you can visit. Go with your family or with some classmates to see the stars and the exhibits. Present a report to your class about what you learned.

ASTRONOMY CLUB MEETING

Many people who are interested in space science join astronomy clubs. They do so to explore the universe and meet with others who share their interest. Such clubs may meet to observe a meteor shower or an eclipse, to share information on building telescopes, or to take photographs of interesting objects in the sky. Contact a local astronomy club. Ask if you can go to a meeting and an observing session. Tell your class about your visit.

BOOKS TO READ

Wings: The Last Book of the Bromeliad

by Terry Pratchett (Delacorte Press, 1990). Be careful! In this book, you'll read about tiny people called *nomes,* who live everywhere. Their leaders have discovered that nomes originally traveled on a spaceship that is now on the moon. Because life on Earth has become dangerous for them, they want to get their spaceship back so they can escape. Will they achieve their goal?

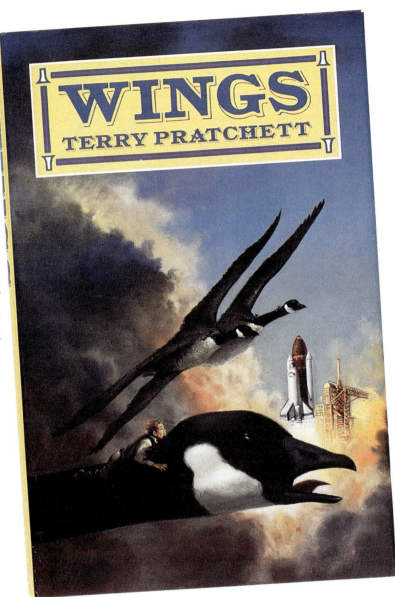

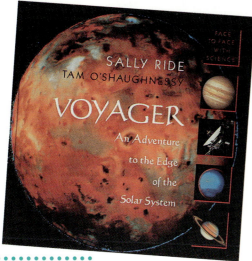

Voyager: An Adventure to the Edge of the Solar System

by Sally Ride and Tam O'Shaughnessy (Crown, 1992), Outstanding Science Trade Book. Would you like to travel in space for 12 years? You would visit four giant planets that had never been visited before. You would pass through the dangerous asteroid belt. Even astronauts cannot take this trip, but two robot spacecraft did. See the amazing pictures they sent back.

More Books to Read

The Big Dipper and You

by E. C. Krupp (William Morrow, 1989), Outstanding Science Trade Book. For hundreds of years, people all over the world have used the Big Dipper as a guide to the sky. Reading about the Big Dipper in this book will help you learn about the stars in the sky.

Could You Ever Meet an Alien?

by David Darling (Dillon Press, 1990). Some scientists hypothesize that if there were intelligent life in outer space, we would have found evidence of it by now. Other scientists hypothesize there could be planets with life on them that we don't even know about. What do you think? This book will help you decide.

Galileo and the Universe

by Steve Parker (HarperCollins, 1992), Outstanding Science Trade Book. Galileo was a mathematician, a physicist, and an astronomer who lived 400 years ago in Italy. In a time when you could be executed for asking questions, he risked his life to carry out scientific experiments and to use mathematics to study the results. Read about this brave scientist and his discoveries.

Raven's Light: A Myth from the People of the Northwest Coast

by Susan Hand Shetterly (Atheneum, 1991). For the ancient people of the Northwest coast of North America, life was hard and uncertain. When they made up stories to explain the world around them, they made Raven, a tricky, clever bird, the creator of the world. Raven made the Earth, but he needed light. How Raven steals the sun from the Kingdom of the Day is told in this book.

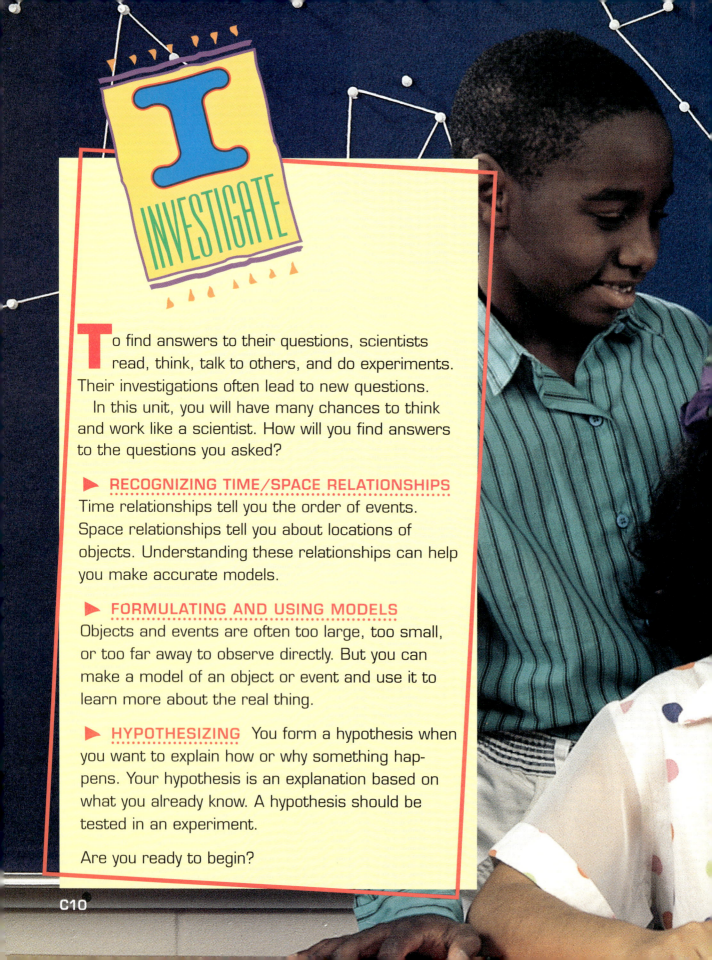

I INVESTIGATE

To find answers to their questions, scientists read, think, talk to others, and do experiments. Their investigations often lead to new questions.

In this unit, you will have many chances to think and work like a scientist. How will you find answers to the questions you asked?

▶ **RECOGNIZING TIME/SPACE RELATIONSHIPS**
Time relationships tell you the order of events. Space relationships tell you about locations of objects. Understanding these relationships can help you make accurate models.

▶ **FORMULATING AND USING MODELS**
Objects and events are often too large, too small, or too far away to observe directly. But you can make a model of an object or event and use it to learn more about the real thing.

▶ **HYPOTHESIZING** You form a hypothesis when you want to explain how or why something happens. Your hypothesis is an explanation based on what you already know. A hypothesis should be tested in an experiment.

Are you ready to begin?

SECTIONS

Going Around Together

▲ The Moon

Have you ever wished you could be an astronaut? Well, in a way, you already are. The Earth itself is like a giant "starbase" traveling around our star, the sun. At the same time, the moon is in orbit around us.

How do the movements of the Earth and the moon in relation to the sun affect you? What do people measure by the movements? In your Science Log, identify three things you find out about StarBase Earth as you work through the investigations that follow.

1 MOVING RIGHT ALONG

People have always wondered about the lights that move across the sky. The two brightest lights are our sun and our moon. In the activities and readings that follow, you will find out about the movements of the Earth-moon-sun system.

ACTIVITY

Out of Sight!

MATERIALS
- small toy ship
- tabletop
- beach ball
- Science Log data sheet

Most ancient people thought Earth was flat. They feared they would sail off the edge. Others thought it was a sphere, like a ball. In this activity, you can test their ideas about the Earth's shape.

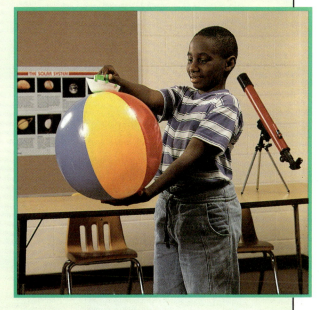

DO THIS

❶ Squat or kneel beside the table or desk. Push the toy ship away from you across the surface until it falls off the other side.

❷ Hold the ball in one hand at eye level. Use your other hand to hold the ship on the surface of the ball. Push the ship away from you across the curve of the ball. Keep holding the ship as it disappears from sight.

THINK AND WRITE

1. What shape do you think the Earth has? Explain how using the two models led you to your conclusion.

2. What happened to the ship as it moved across the ball? Describe its appearance.

So Near, So Far

Like the Earth, the moon and the sun are sphere-shaped. Ancient people noticed that the moon and the sun appeared to be about the same size in the sky. They did not know the actual diameters of the moon and the sun. How could two such different objects appear to be the same size?

MATERIALS
- tennis ball
- smaller ball
- Science Log data sheet

DO THIS

1 Set the tennis ball on a desk.

2 Hold the smaller ball in your outstretched hand in front of you.

3 Slowly back away from the tennis ball. With each step, stop and line up the two balls so that they appear to be next to each other. Observe the apparent sizes of the balls.

THINK AND WRITE

1. What happened to the apparent sizes of the two balls?

2. Why do you think the moon and the sun appear to be the same size?

3. **RECOGNIZING TIME/SPACE RELATIONSHIPS**
Space relationships can tell you about locations of objects. How did the model you used help you discover the space relationship that affects the apparent sizes of the moon and the sun?

From Myth to Science

To some ancient people, the moon was the hunting goddess Diana. To us, it is the Earth's natural satellite. As you read, think about how ancient people made the leap from telling stories about the universe to scientifically describing how it works.

Early people had no binoculars, telescopes, or computers. They did not even have eyeglasses. However, they were astronomers, or careful observers of the universe. They made very accurate records and predictions based upon its movements. But they did not know what the objects they studied were.

A myth is a story created to explain something in nature. Early people made up myths about the moon, the sun, and the stars. The moon, for example, was said to be good for farmers because its light did not burn the Earth the way the sun's did. So some people created stories about the moon as the goddess of farming. Others saw that there was a connection between the moon and the tides. So they made up stories that featured the moon as the goddess of the sea.

About 2,500 years ago, some Greek astronomers began to seek other ways to explain the universe. They used ways that did not depend upon myths. They observed, measured, and reasoned to try to understand the universe.

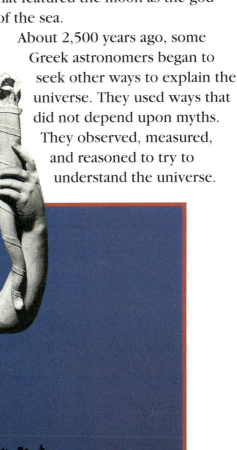

Goddess Diana ▶

Aristarchus (air ihs TAHR kuhs), for example, looked at the Earth's shadow on the moon during an eclipse. He concluded that the sun was much larger than the Earth and that it was much farther away than other people thought. He decided that the sun must be at the center of the universe.

"The Earth and the other planets *orbit*, or revolve around the sun," he said. People laughed. Anybody could see that the Earth remained still while everything else moved around it!

Aristarchus also calculated the distance from the Earth to the sun. He used sound methods of measurement, but came up with 8,000,000 kilometers (49.6 million miles). This is much less than the actual distance—150 million kilometers (93 million miles).

Eratosthenes (er uh TAHS thuh neez), another Greek scientist, calculated the Earth's circumference. He did so by measuring the sun's angle at the summer solstice, the time of longest daylight.

Anaximander (uh NAKS uh man duhr) made a timekeeper. First, he stuck a stick into the ground. Then, he watched the stick's shadow change during the day. He made accurate measurements to mark the times of daylight, the times of the seasons, and the length of the year.

THINK ABOUT IT

How is what the Greek scientists did to explain things in the universe different from what the storytellers did?

▼ Earth's movements change the appearance of shadows during the day.

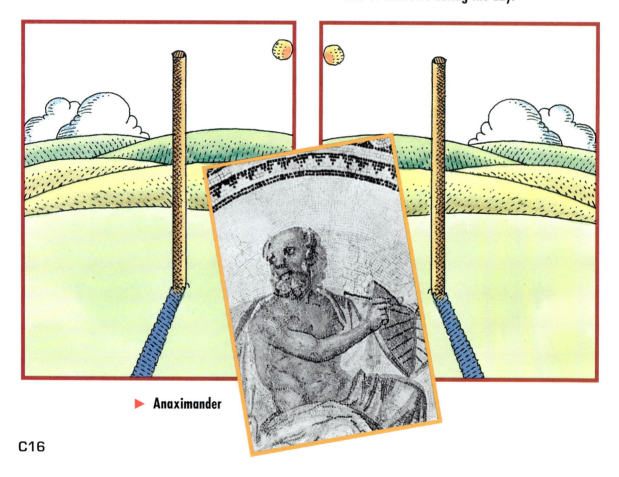

▶ Anaximander

ACTIVITY

That's Stretching It!

As the centuries passed, more and more people began to realize that the Earth and the other planets travel around the sun. It seemed to them that the path the planets took around the sun is a circle. Is it? Complete the activity to find out.

DO THIS

1 Stick one pushpin into the center of the cardboard. Stick the other one in about 5 cm away in any direction.

2 Loop the string and tie the ends together. Now put the string around the pushpins.

3 Put your pencil inside the loop and stretch out the string with the pencil point. Keep the string tight and move the pencil around the pushpins.

4 Move the pushpins farther apart and draw the path of the pencil. Move them closer together and draw the path of the pencil.

THINK AND WRITE

1. What kind of shape did you draw? How did the shape change when you moved the pushpins farther apart? closer together? The shape of the Earth's orbit is similar to the shape you would draw if you moved the pushpins very close together.

2. **FORMULATING AND USING MODELS**
   In this activity, you made and used a model to understand the shape of the Earth's orbit around the sun. Suppose one pushpin represents the sun and the pencil's path represents the Earth's orbit. What can you conclude about the Earth's distance from the sun as it orbits the sun?

The Face in the Moon

Have you seen the giant "face" in the moon? Each night when the moon is almost full, the same face appears. Why do we see only one side of the moon? Modeling the moon's spin and orbit will help you answer this question.

Place a chair where you can walk around it. Start circling the chair in a counterclockwise direction. When you are halfway around, notice which side of your body is visible from the chair. Is it your left side or your right side? Notice the position of your body again when you are three-fourths of the way around. Also check it when you complete the circle. Has the right side of your body ever been the side closer to the chair?

What can you infer about the moon's rate of spin in relation to its rate of orbiting the Earth? Now you should know why you always see the same face in the moon.

THINK ABOUT IT

Is the far side of the moon always dark? Explain.

▶ Can you see the face?

▼ This is the moon's far side, photographed by *Luna 3*.

Watch Where You're Going!

The Earth, the moon, and the sun have many movements you can observe. As you discovered in a previous activity, the Earth moves around the sun in a not quite circular path. This path is called an *ellipse*. Complete this activity to see how the movements all fit together.

MATERIALS
- beach ball
- volleyball
- tennis ball
- Science Log data sheet

DO THIS

1 Hold the beach ball (the sun). Have a classmate hold the volleyball (Earth) some distance from the sun. Have another classmate hold the tennis ball (the moon) near the Earth.

2 First, the volleyball must spin the way the Earth spins in place. Next, the moon must orbit the Earth in an ellipse. The classmate holding the tennis ball must always keep the same side of the ball toward the Earth. Finally, as these things are going on, the Earth must slowly orbit the sun in an ellipse.

THINK AND WRITE

Which movement takes the least time—the Earth spinning once, the moon orbiting once around the Earth, or the Earth orbiting once around the sun? Which movement takes the most time? Explain.

A Heavy Subject

When you asked your **I Wonder** questions, did you wonder why you don't fall off the Earth? Did you ask why the moon stays in orbit around the Earth? Read about a famous scientist who wondered about these same things.

Isaac Newton lived about three centuries ago. He had one of the greatest minds in the history of science. Newton invented a new form of math. He discovered the range of colors in visible light. He invented the reflecting telescope

and formulated the basic laws of motion. Finally, as if that were not enough, Newton discovered gravity!

Newton wondered about the moon and its orbit. Why, he asked, did the moon not fly off into space along its own path? According to one story, one day he was sitting in his mother's garden, and he watched an apple fall to the ground.

Suddenly, he had an idea. What if the force that caused the apple to fall to the Earth was the same force that kept the moon in orbit?

▼ **Sir Isaac Newton**

▶ **Newton's telescope**

Newton thought and thought. He was very good at this! He finally came up with the law of universal gravitation. The law says that all bodies in the universe are attracted to all other bodies. This attraction among bodies is **gravity.** The greater the mass—or the amount of matter—of each body, the stronger the attraction. Gravity affects all objects in the universe.

Newton's law explains why the apple falls to Earth. It also explains why the moon is attracted to the Earth and why the Earth is attracted to the sun. Each body acts on the other through the force of gravity. Try the following activity to model the Earth in orbit around the sun.

You will need: safety goggles, a 1-m long string and a key

 CAUTION: Put on safety goggles.

Securely tie a long piece of string to a key. In an open area, away from your classmates, carefully swing the key around your head. What do you feel from the key as you swing it? What path does the key take? What would happen if the string suddenly broke?

THINK ABOUT IT

Why do you think the sun's gravity does not pull the Earth into the sun?

▼ **Orbits of Earth and moon**

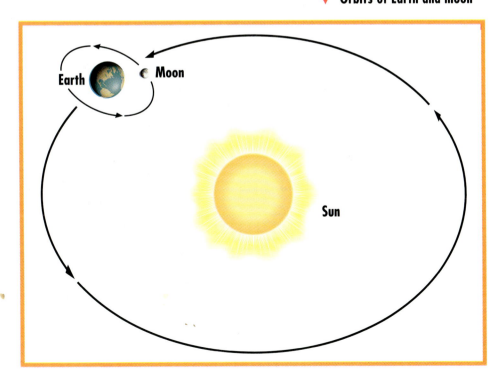

Casting Shadows

You might think that with so many objects in the universe orbiting one another, they would cross each other's paths. Well, they do. In the following activity, you will see how the sun and the moon can be darkened, or *eclipsed.*

DO THIS

1 Darken the classroom.

2 Shine the flashlight (the sun) on the wall.

3 Hold the basketball (Earth) between the sun's light and the wall to show the Earth's shadow.

4 Move the tennis ball (the moon) between the Earth and the wall. Observe what happens.

5 Move the tennis ball between the basketball and the light. Observe what happens.

THINK AND WRITE

1. Which action represented an eclipse of the moon?

2. Which action represented an eclipse of the sun?

3. Why does an eclipse of the moon throw the entire moon into shadow? Why does an eclipse of the sun throw only a partial shadow on the Earth?

4. Look at the photograph. Why do you think that the moon is not completely eclipsing the sun?

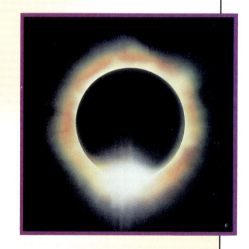

You're Blocking My View!

Ancient astronomers observed and tried to predict eclipses, even if they did not understand them. Read on to see what these people thought was going on in the sky.

The people of many early cultures were frightened by eclipses of the sun and the moon. Some believed that these events were battles between heavenly beings.

The Miwok people of what is now California thought that eclipses were fights between the sun and the moon. The Pomo, also of California, believed that a great bear was walking along the Milky Way and met the sun. The sun would not let the bear pass. So the two fought! The sun was eclipsed when the bear won.

In Viking mythology, wolves tried to eat the sun and the moon and blotted them out. The Chinese believed that the sun's enemy was a dragon. For the Maya, it was a large, fanged snake.

Ancient people would often sing, dance, and make loud noises to scare away these "evil spirits." They thought that this restored the moon and the sun to their rightful place in the heavens.

Why did people's noise and singing always seem to work? What would happen after a period of time?

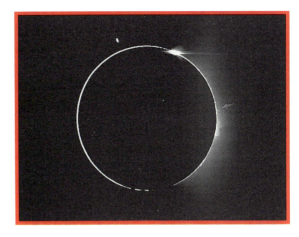

▲ **Solar eclipse**   ▼ **Lunar eclipse**

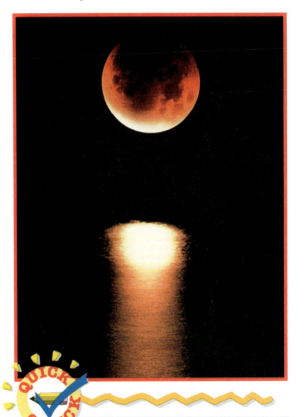

LESSON 1 REVIEW

❶ Describe the movements of the Earth and the moon in relation to the sun.

❷ What are some beliefs ancient people had about the sun and the moon?

2 WHAT TIME IS IT?

You've explored the movements of the Earth around the sun and of the moon around the Earth. When viewed from the Earth, these movements occur in regular patterns. Throughout history, people have kept time by these patterns. What patterns can be used to mark the passing of time?

Ancient Astronomers

Astronomy is the oldest science. It began even before written language. People needed to understand the cycle of changes on Earth. Then they could plant and harvest crops, sail safely by sea, and do other important activities. Many ancient people built stone structures and kept calendars as ways to mark the changing skies.

The Babylonians lived in what is present-day Iraq around 3000 B.C. The Babylonians viewed the universe as a disk of land surrounded by water, with Babylon in the center.

About 5,000 years ago, a kind of observatory was built in Britain. It is called *Stonehenge.* Stonehenge is similar to earlier observatories built in Egypt and South America. The builders of Stonehenge arranged huge stones so that the rays of the rising sun would shine through openings between the stones at certain important times of the year. Thus, Stonehenge may have been a kind of calendar.

El Caracol was a Mayan observatory. Astronomers observed Venus through openings in the top of this structure.

The Anasazi (ahn uh SAH zee) lived in the American Southwest about A.D. 1000. They marked the movements of the moon, the sun, and the stars. Casa Rincañada is an Anasazi kiva, or holy place. It lies in a perfect east-west line.

The Arabs of the Middle East preserved many astronomical records during the Middle Ages. The Arabs also refined the *astrolabe,* an instrument for measuring the altitude of the sun and stars.

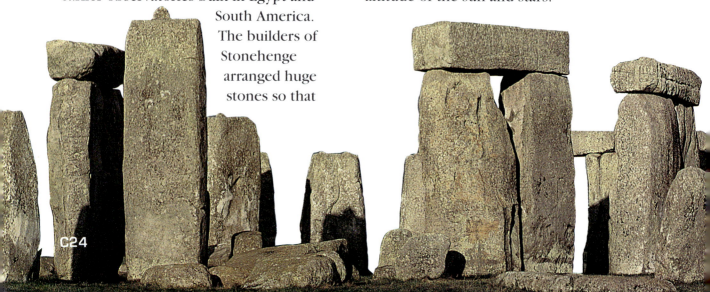

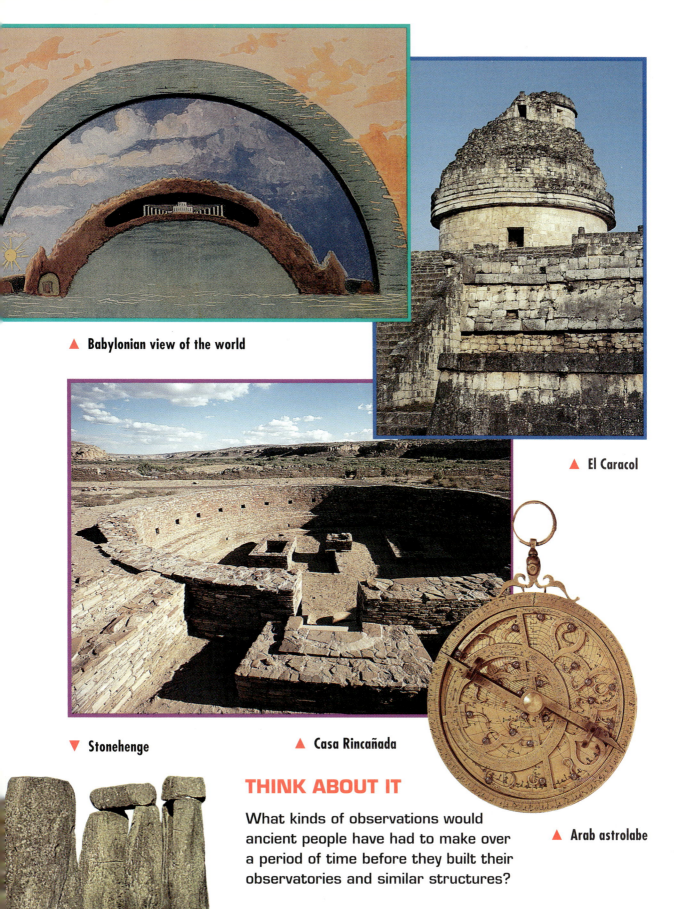

▲ Babylonian view of the world

▲ El Caracol

▼ Stonehenge

▲ Casa Rincañada

THINK ABOUT IT

What kinds of observations would ancient people have had to make over a period of time before they built their observatories and similar structures?

▲ Arab astrolabe

ACTIVITY

A Long Day's Journey

Once people recognized that the apparent movements of the sun and moon happened over and over, they began to use these cycles to organize their lives. The following activity will help you see why there is always another day.

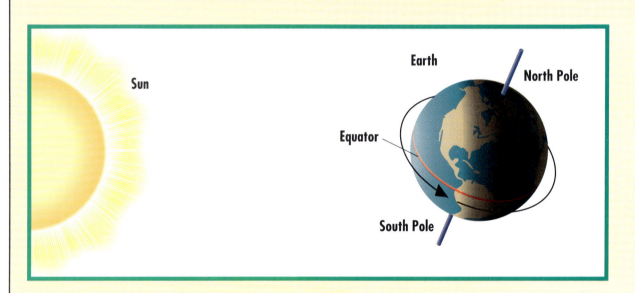

DO THIS

1. Cut out a strip of paper and write your community's name on it. Tape it to the globe in approximately the correct place.

2. Darken the room.

3. Shine the flashlight on the globe.

4. Rotate the globe in a counter-clockwise direction as seen from above.

THINK AND WRITE

1. What cycle did you just model? Describe it.

2. How does this cycle affect humans, other animals, and plants?

A Seasonal Change

The Earth's rotation causes the cycle of night and day. What kind of cycle does the Earth's *revolution,* or trip around the sun, cause? Find out in this activity.

MATERIALS
• Earth globe tilted on its axis
• large flashlight
• Science Log data sheet

DO THIS

❶ Shine the flashlight (sun) directly on a spot on the globe and then at a slant on the same spot. Record your observations.

❷ Hold the globe while someone else shines the light directly on the equator.

❸ Rotate the globe slowly while you move around the person with the light. Keep the globe tilted toward the same side of the room. The person with the light should also turn, keeping the light on the equator.

THINK AND WRITE

1. In steps 1 and 2, which was larger—the area in the path of the direct rays or the area with the slanted rays?

2. Which form of the sun's rays—direct or slanted—do you think is brighter and hotter?

3. When the sun's slanted rays hit the Northern Hemisphere, which season does your community have?

4. When the sun's slanted rays hit the Southern Hemisphere, which season do you have?

5. What do we call each of the Earth's revolutions around the sun? How long is it?

The Long and Short of It

You know that there are more hours of daylight in the summer and more hours of darkness in the winter. Why is this so?

The lengths of daylight and darkness in a place depend on two things. They are the time of year and how far from the equator the place is.

Because the Earth is tilted, the amount of sunlight any place receives changes as the Earth moves around the sun. During our summer, the Northern Hemisphere tilts toward the sun. Then we have long days and short nights. As the Earth continues its orbit, the Southern Hemisphere tilts toward the sun. This gives people there long days and short nights, while we have just the opposite. This is our winter.

The day with the most sunlight, June 20 or 21, is called the *summer solstice.* The day with the most darkness, December 21 or 22, is the *winter solstice.* March 20 or 21 and September 22 or 23 are the two days halfway between the solstices. They are called the spring and fall *equinoxes. Equinox* comes from a word that means "equal night."

THINK ABOUT IT

Which parts of the Earth always have days and nights of about equal length? Which parts regularly have very long days or very long nights? Explain.

▼ **Earth's tilt and its orbit around the sun cause the seasons.**

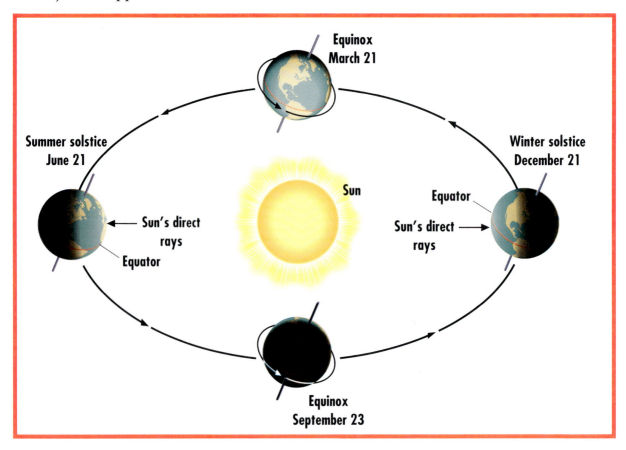

Equinox
March 21

Summer solstice
June 21

Sun's direct rays

Equator

Sun

Winter solstice
December 21

Equator

Sun's direct rays

Equinox
September 23

Land of the Midnight Sun

The polar areas are the most affected by the Earth's tilt. Each pole receives months of continuous daylight followed by months of continuous darkness. What is life like in these areas?

Norway is a European country that lies above the Arctic Circle. It is called the Land of the Midnight Sun because the sun shines almost all of the time during the summer.

In Norway, children attend school in the dark from mid-November through January because the sun does not shine at all. But in the summer they go to bed while it is light, from mid-May through July.

After months of darkness, children in Norway get a day's vacation from school in late January to greet the returning sun. The continuous darkness in the winter causes some people to feel sad. So Norwegians are always delighted by the appearance of the *northern lights* when the sun doesn't shine.

THINK ABOUT IT

How would periods of daylight and darkness in the Antarctic compare to those periods in the Arctic Circle?

The northern lights

It's Just a Phase!

Perhaps you have watched the moon go through *phases*, or changes in its appearance. A new cycle of phases begins about every 29 days. Why do you think this happens? Now try this activity to test your ideas.

DO THIS

❶ Darken the room and turn on the lamp.

❷ Stand with your back to the lamp.

❸ Hold the ball at arm's length above your head so that it is in the light.

❹ Rotate counterclockwise, keeping the ball in the same position. Stop each eighth of the way around and draw a picture that shows how much of the ball appears lit.

THINK AND WRITE

1. What did the lamp represent? the ball?

2. Describe how much of the lighted half of the ball you could see and your position at each stopping point in your rotation. What is each similar phase of the moon called?

3. Now what do you think causes the cycle of phases of the moon? Compare your answer with your first idea.

4. What period of time on a calendar is nearly the same as the time it takes the moon to orbit the Earth?

The Moon's Got Pull, Too!

Suppose you visit a beach at the nearest ocean. What effect of the moon's gravitational attraction on the Earth would you see? Read the following and you'll see that the moon's phases are related to another cycle of change.

The Earth's force of gravity keeps the moon in orbit. However, the moon's gravitation has an effect on the Earth, too. It causes the twice-daily cycle of tides in the Earth's oceans.

When the moon's gravity pulls on the Earth's oceans, it causes them to bulge. This causes high tides on the side of the Earth facing the moon, as well as on the opposite side. The areas in between have low tides. As the Earth rotates, different places have high and low tides.

Twice each month, at the new moon and full moon, the sun and moon line up with the Earth. This causes higher and lower tides than usual. These are called *spring tides*. *Neap tides* occur twice a month also, at the quarter moons, when the sun and the moon form a right angle with the Earth. Neap tides are moderate in height.

Spring tides ▼

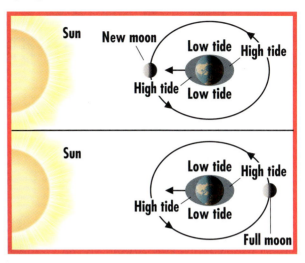

Neap tides ▼

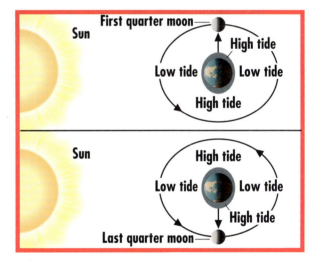

LESSON 2 REVIEW

❶ What effect of the Earth's rotation do we observe?

❷ Suppose the only night you see the moon, it is half lit. How can you tell whether the full moon or the new moon phase is approaching?

3 A TRAVELER'S GUIDE TO THE MOON

Long before the astronauts set foot on the moon, astronomers had mapped it more completely than some parts of Africa had been mapped. We have learned even more from the *Apollo* space missions. On the following pages you will find out what the moon is really like.

Don't Go Out Without a Suit!

Why do astronauts have to wear spacesuits on the moon? Read the following to see what you could and could not do on the moon.

On July 20, 1969, humans stood on the moon for the first time. After landing the lunar module *Eagle,* astronauts Neil Armstrong and Edwin "Buzz" Aldrin stepped out on the surface. For two and one-half hours they collected rocks and soil. They set up experiments and took pictures. Armstrong took this one of Aldrin.

▶ *"That's one small step . . ."*

The moon has a very limited atmosphere. There is no oxygen to breathe and not enough atmosphere to even out the temperature. As a result, the moon's surface is very hot during its day and then freezing during its night. The moon's day and night are both about two Earth weeks long. You would be very glad to have a spacesuit there.

▲ The Apollo astronauts were able to leap easily on the moon. They weighed only one-sixth of their Earth weight.

▲ This is the first image of the moon's thin atmosphere.

On the other hand, you would enjoy running and jumping on the moon. It has one-sixth the gravity of Earth, so you would weigh only one-sixth of what you weigh on Earth. Think how easy it would be to slam-dunk a basketball! But remember, you'd have to do it while wearing a spacesuit.

THINK ABOUT IT

Imagine how large a baseball stadium would have to be if you could hit a ball six times farther than on Earth! How would some of your favorite sports change on the moon?

C33

Scope It Out!

People used to think that the surface of the moon was flat and smooth. Read to find out what the moon's surface is really like.

The moon is about the same age as Earth, four and one-half billion years. Some scientists think that when Earth was young, a large body hit it and exploded. The explosion hurled a lot of debris into space. The Earth's gravity captured the debris, which became the moon.

Scientists can find out the relative ages of features on the moon. Large rocks hit the moon long ago, so areas with many craters are the oldest. Volcanoes erupted because the impacts heated up the moon, melting some of the surface, so the smooth areas, called maria, are younger. Craters that sit inside maria are younger than the maria. Also, any crater that partly covers another crater is younger. This is because the rock that produced it had to hit the moon's surface more recently than did the rock that produced the crater underneath it.

▲ The jagged edge of the sun-and-shadow line across the moon proved to observers that its surface has varying heights.

▼ Surface of the moon

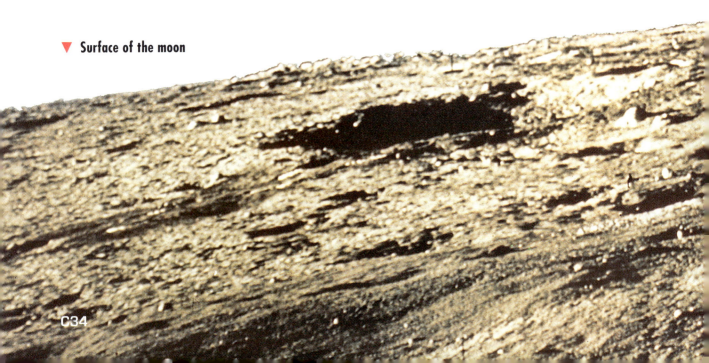

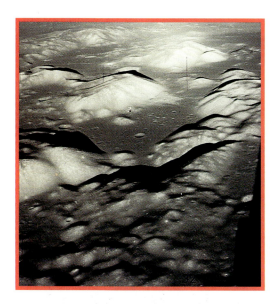

▲ About 85 percent of the moon's surface is light-colored highlands. These were formed by the continuous impact of meteorites. The tallest mountains are only 6,100 meters (20,000 feet) high. They erode very slowly because there is no weather on the moon.

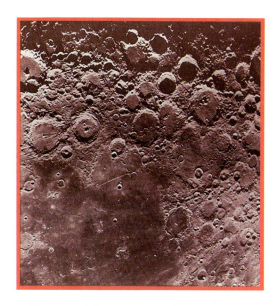

▲ The rest of the moon's surface is *maria,* which means "seas." Early observers thought these areas contained water. They are actually craters that were filled with lava during the moon's volcanic period.

LESSON 3 REVIEW

What area of the moon would you choose to explore? Describe what you would expect to find.

DOUBLE CHECK

SECTION A REVIEW

1. Why do the sun and the moon appear to be about the same size?

2. What patterns can be used to mark the passing of time? Describe and explain each one.

3. Compare the features of the Earth and the moon.

Close to Home

▲ Planetary space probe

The size of the universe is hard to imagine. Most of us feel more comfortable learning about it by starting with our own solar system. Each member of our solar system was probably formed from the same gas and dust. Yet each member is very different from all the others.

In this section, you will investigate each member of the solar system one by one. Think of three facts you now know about our solar system, and write them in your Science Log. Add to your notes as you work through the investigations of StarBase Earth's neighborhood.

1 OUR NEIGHBORHOOD

Our neighbors in space are the sun, a family of 8 other planets, about 70 known moons, and many comets and asteroids. Together with the Earth, these objects form one vast, continuously moving *solar system.* Its scale and structure will amaze you.

Wrong-Way Planet

Long ago, astronomers observing the night sky saw that some points of light do not always move in the same direction as the others. One of these points of light, the planet Mars, seems to move backward at times. That is, it appears to move from west to east over several nights, instead of from east to west. Does Mars really move backward? Try this activity and decide for yourself.

You will need: a large open space

Ask a classmate to begin walking slowly in a circle. Then, moments later, begin walking in the same direction in a circle. Make sure your circle has the same center but a slightly smaller radius. Now speed up so that you pass your classmate. How does his or her movement appear to change against the background as you pass by?

▼ **Mars**

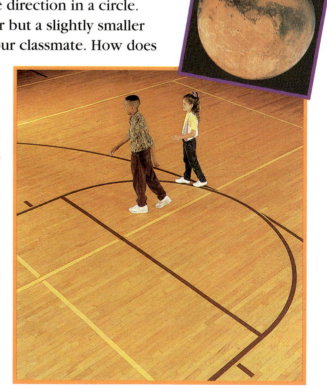

Scientists think that the solar system formed about 4.5 billion years ago from a swirling cloud of dust and gas. As this gas cloud condensed to form the sun, it began to spin in one direction. Some of the gas and dust that was thrown off formed the planets. That's why all the planets orbit the sun in the same direction, even though sometimes this doesn't seem to be so.

THINK ABOUT IT

Does Mars really move backward? Explain.

The Big Picture

What do we know about the planets? The pictures on these pages will give you some information about the members of our solar system.

Because the distances in the solar system are so large, astronomers use a measurement called an AU. AU stands for astronomical unit, the distance between the Earth and the sun, or 150 million kilometers (93 million miles).

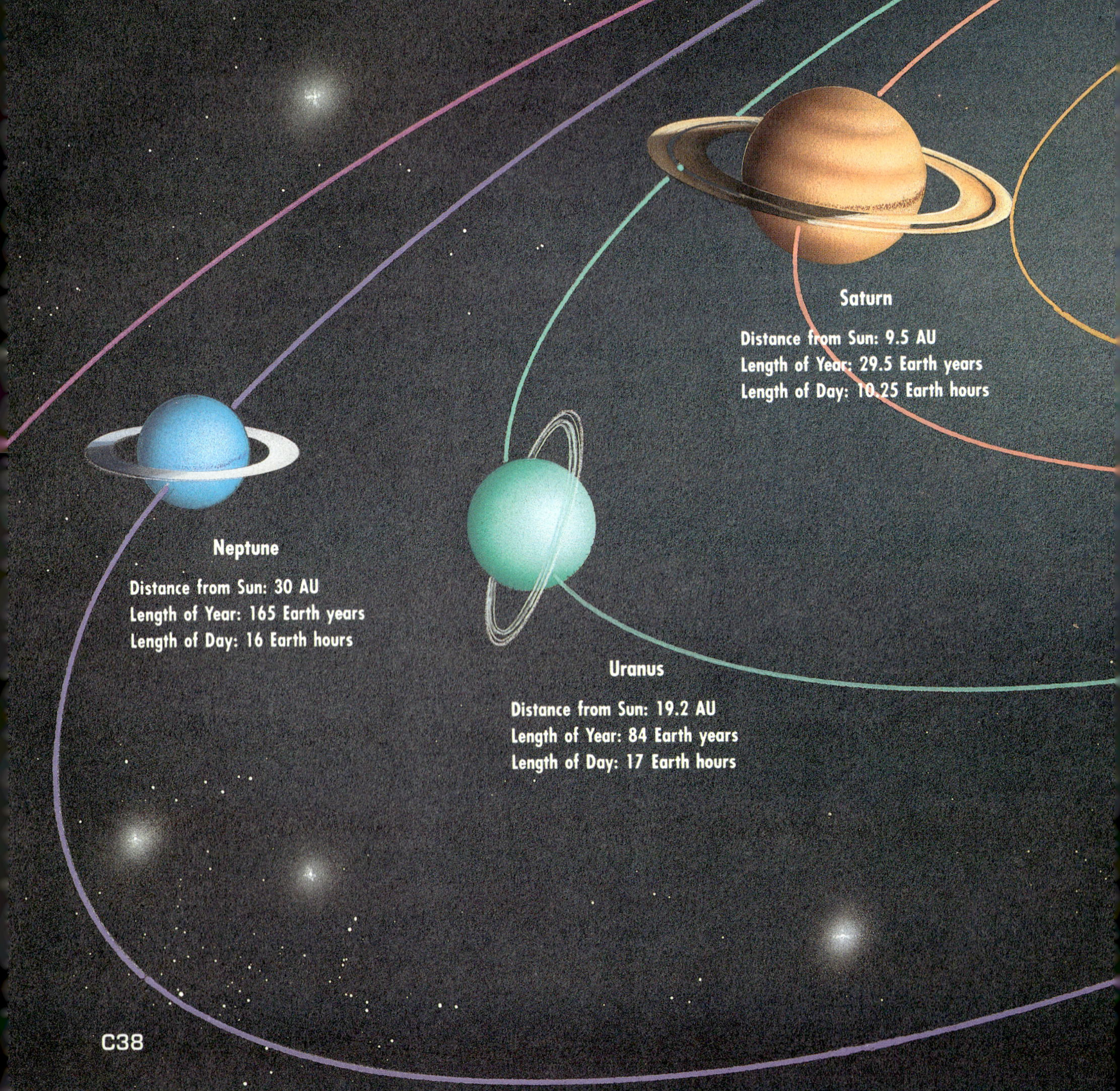

Saturn

Distance from Sun: 9.5 AU
Length of Year: 29.5 Earth years
Length of Day: 10.25 Earth hours

Neptune

Distance from Sun: 30 AU
Length of Year: 165 Earth years
Length of Day: 16 Earth hours

Uranus

Distance from Sun: 19.2 AU
Length of Year: 84 Earth years
Length of Day: 17 Earth hours

Mercury

Distance from Sun:
0.40 AU
Length of Year:
88 Earth days
Length of Day:
59 Earth days

Venus

Distance from Sun:
0.72 AU
Length of Year:
225 Earth days
Length of Day:
243 Earth days

Jupiter

Distance from Sun: 5.2 AU
Length of Year: 11.9 Earth years
Length of Day: 9.8 Earth hours

Earth

Distance from Sun: 1 AU
Length of Year: 365.26 days
Length of Day: 24 hours

Mars

Distance from Sun: 1.5 AU
Length of Year: 1.9 Earth years
Length of Day: 24.5 Earth hours

Pluto

Distance from Sun: 39.5 AU
Length of Year: 248 Earth years
Length of Day: 6.4 Earth days

THINK ABOUT IT

Compare the facts given for the nine planets. What patterns can you find?

Let's Scale It Down!

Scientists make scale models to help them understand the real world. Models are especially helpful for studying the solar system because it's so large. In this activity, you can make a model of planet distances from the sun.

DO THIS

1 Use construction paper, colored pencils, and scissors to draw and cut out a large circular sun. Tape the sun on one end of the wall.

2 Use the scale 10 cm = 1 AU. Draw and cut out a paper Earth, and tape it 10 cm from the edge of the sun.

3 Draw, cut out, position, and tape the other eight planets in place, using the same scale. Refer to pages C38–C39 for the distances of the planets from the sun. Round off the number of astronomical units to make your figuring easier.

THINK AND WRITE

▶ **RECOGNIZING TIME/SPACE RELATIONSHIPS** In this activity, you used a scale to show a space relationship between the real planet distances from the sun and the distances on your model. Why was it important to always measure the distance from the sun instead of from one planet to another?

QUICK CHECK

LESSON 1 REVIEW

1 When seen from Earth, which planets would never appear to move backward in the sky? Explain.

2 How would you describe the way the planets are arranged in the solar system?

INNER PLANETS AND ASTEROIDS

The four planets closest to the sun—Mercury, Venus, Earth, and Mars—are called the *inner planets.* You will discover that these planets, along with the asteroids, have something in common.

Mercury and Venus

The United States' *Mariner 10* and *Magellan* space probes showed us the surfaces of Mercury and Venus. See and read what was discovered.

Mercury, the closest planet to the sun, is about the size of Earth's moon. A crust and a deeper rocky layer surround a huge core of iron and nickel. The surface temperature varies from –180°C to 430°C (–292°F to 806°F). The planet is not large enough for its gravity to hold onto a moon or much of an atmosphere.

Venus, about the size of Earth, is made of rock that covers a core of iron. But we're not likely to walk on the surface of Venus, because the atmosphere is dense and hot 465°C (869°F), and contains carbon dioxide and sulfuric acid! We would be burned, suffocated, cooked, and crushed! Venus has no moon but may have active volcanoes.

The *Magellan* spacecraft used radar imaging to cut through Venus's cloudy atmosphere. The dark areas indicate smooth ground, and the light areas indicate rough ground.

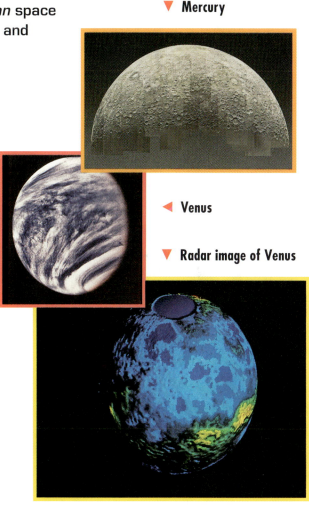

▼ **Mercury**

◄ **Venus**

▼ **Radar image of Venus**

THINK ABOUT IT

What other body in the solar system does Mercury look like? Explain.

Earth

Mercury and Venus are too hot and dry to support life. Find out what makes Earth the right place for life. See how photographs from space show this.

Earth has a solid inner core surrounded by a liquid outer core, a rocky mantle, and a crust. The planet has volcanic eruptions and earthquakes. Sunlight, a nitrogen- and oxygen-rich atmosphere, large oceans, and the greenhouse effect make climates that support life.

A Watery World
Almost two-thirds of Earth's surface is covered by water. Without water, there could be no life as we know it.

Weather Patterns
Sunlight, the atmosphere, and ocean currents create Earth's weather.

Atmosphere
Earth's atmosphere provides air to breathe. It protects life from harmful solar radiation.

Ozone Holes
A layer of ozone (a form of oxygen) surrounds the Earth. Ozone protects us from harmful ultraviolet rays. Recently, the ozone has thinned out over both poles and in other places.

Polar Ice
Large, growing sheets of ice cover the polar regions. These regions receive the least amount of direct sunlight.

THINK ABOUT IT

Why do you think that Earth is the only inner planet that has life?

Guy Bluford:

Space-Shuttle Astronaut

Satellites provide us with much information about Earth. But human observations and research in space are important also. Guy Bluford knows firsthand about space research. He is a former space-shuttle astronaut.

After graduation from The Pennsylvania State University, Bluford became an Air Force pilot and an aerospace engineer. He became interested in astronaut training when the space shuttle was being developed. The Air Force gave him the opportunity to apply for the space program, and he did so in 1977. He was accepted and immediately began training for his first mission.

Bluford's job on space-shuttle flights was mission-specialist astronaut. Mission specialists run various experiments on board an orbiting space shuttle. In addition to running the experiments, Bluford had to fix the equipment if something broke.

Most space-shuttle experiments can be divided into two categories: materials-processing experiments and life-science experiments. Materials-processing experiments involve making materials, such as computer chips or medicines, in the near-zero gravity of space. Some life-science experiments involve studying plants in orbit, to observe how near-zero gravity affects plant growth.

Mission specialists run many different experiments during a space-shuttle flight. Bluford would sometimes have as many as 75 experiments working at the same time. Learning everything necessary to complete so many experiments successfully is the most challenging part of the job.

In the future, mission specialists will be needed to run experiments on America's orbiting space station. The space station will be a permanent laboratory where scientists will learn even more about Earth.

THINK ABOUT IT

How do mission-specialist astronauts help us learn more about Earth?

C43

Mars and the Asteroids

Of all the planets, Mars and some asteroids are the most likely to be explored and settled by humans. Read to see why this may someday be possible.

Mars is the most Earth-like planet in our solar system. It has a small, solid, iron core. The surface has mountains, deserts, volcanoes, and canyons. A thin atmosphere of carbon dioxide covers the surface. On a Martian day, temperatures may range from a freezing –120°C (–184°F) to a comfortable 25°C (77°F). In 1976 two NASA Viking Landers tested the Martian soil for signs of life and found none.

▲ Mars has the longest canyon in the solar system. Valles Marineris, shown here, is about the width of the United States. The channel-like features suggest that Mars once had running water. There may still be water frozen under the polar areas.

▲ Mars, about half the size of Earth, is large enough to hold onto two moons, Phobos and Deimos. They are oddly shaped objects and may be captured asteroids.

▲ Olympus Mons is the largest volcano in the solar system. It stands three times as high as Mount Everest.

A wide belt of small objects called *asteroids* orbits the sun between Mars and Jupiter. Asteroids are sometimes called *minor planets*. All of them together would not equal the amount of material in our moon. The largest asteroid is Ceres. Asteroids might be the remains of a planet pulled apart by Jupiter's gravity. Or they might be bits and pieces left over from the formation of the solar system.

The asteroids are rich in minerals, and scientists think about mining them. Larger asteroids may be used as research stations someday.

▲ The spacecraft *Galileo* took this close-up of an asteroid in 1993. It is rocky, like everything else in the inner solar system. Notice the tiny impact craters. What do they tell you about the age of this asteroid?

QUICK CHECK

LESSON 2 REVIEW

Make a table to compare the inner planets. Use headings such as *Size*, *Temperature*, and *Atmosphere*.

3 OUTER PLANETS, COMETS, AND METEORS

From 1977 to 1989, two *Voyager* spacecraft flew by the four large outer planets. The photographs and data collected by the *Voyagers* showed a group of planets and moons with strange features unlike anything seen among the inner planets. Read on to find out how the outer planets differ from the inner planets.

Jupiter

Beyond the orbits of the four inner planets moves Jupiter, the first outer planet. See and read about what makes Jupiter and its moons so strange.

Jupiter is the largest planet. Its atmosphere is cold hydrogen gas. Below that is liquid hydrogen. Examine Jupiter's features shown on the next page.

Like the other giant outer planets, Jupiter has many moons. The four largest, those discovered long ago by Galileo, are called the *Galilean moons* in his honor. They are named Io, Europa, Ganymede, and Callisto. The Voyager spacecraft found 13 additional moons around Jupiter, bringing the known total to 17.

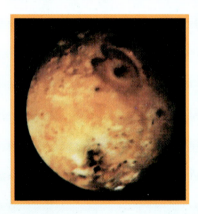

▲ Io is nicknamed "the pizza moon" because of its appearance. Io is one of only two moons in the solar system with active volcanoes.

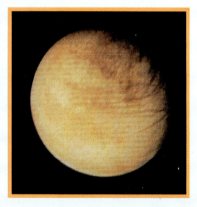

▲ The smooth, icy surface of Europa may hide a huge ocean.

▲ Larger than the planet Mercury, Ganymede has an icy crust with many craters.

North Equatorial Belt
Strong winds blow in opposite directions among cloud belts.

North Temperate Belt
The southern edge is bordered by "red ovals," giant circling movements in the atmosphere.

North Tropical Zone
This bright zone contains high clouds made of ammonia crystals.

Great Red Spot
Jupiter's Great Red Spot is the size of three Earths. Astronomers think it is a giant storm.

▲ Callisto is larger than Earth's moon. It is covered with craters made of ice.

Jupiter's Ring
In January 1979, *Voyager 1* discovered a thin, faint ring made of dark grains of dust.

South Polar Region
Within swirling clouds lie "white ovals," gigantic storm systems.

THINK ABOUT IT

How are Jupiter and its moons different from the inner planets and their moons?

Saturn

Saturn was the farthest of the outer planets known to ancient astronomers. To them, it looked like a pale, yellow light. What is Saturn really like?

Saturn, like Jupiter, is mostly gas, although it is much less dense than Jupiter. In fact, Saturn is so light that it could float on water! Saturn has at least 18 moons, many of them discovered by the two Voyager spacecraft. It also has a large, beautiful system of rings made up of millions of bits of ice.

Encke Division
The innermost moon orbits in the gap between Saturn and its rings.

A Windy Planet
Like Jupiter, Saturn's atmosphere has cloud belts that are blown in opposite directions.

Ring's Edge
The outermost bright ring was discovered in 1979.

Cassini Division
This appeared to be a space between rings. Voyager ships found many faint small rings within the division.

▲ Titan, Saturn's largest moon, is the second largest in the solar system.

THINK ABOUT IT

The appearance of Saturn's rings changes during the planet's orbit. Sometimes we see the topside of the rings. Other times we see their underside. In 1995 and again in 2003, Saturn will appear to be ringless. How will Saturn be facing us during those two years?

Where Is It?

Saturn and all the closer planets can be seen without a telescope. How did astronomers find Uranus, Neptune, and Pluto? Read on to find out.

Uranus was discovered by British astronomer William Herschel in 1781. Herschel also discovered two of the planet's moons and observed that the moons orbit in the same direction that the planet rotates—clockwise.

After Uranus was discovered, astronomers saw that the planet was being pulled off course by the gravity of some unknown body—perhaps another planet. They looked for and found Neptune in 1846.

The odd thing was that Neptune's gravity was not strong enough to affect the orbit of Uranus. So the search went on for Planet X.

American astronomer Percival Lowell began to hunt for Planet X in 1905. He looked at thousands of photographic plates to find an object that moved against the background of stars. But he never found it.

▲ Clyde Tombaugh

◀ Refracting telescope

In 1928 American astronomer Clyde Tombaugh continued the search. Like Lowell, Tombaugh compared many images on photographic plates. In 1930 he found a "star" that had moved a long distance over just six days. Clyde Tombaugh had found Planet X in the area of sky near the constellation Gemini.

THINK ABOUT IT

What other kinds of objects in the solar system could be found by looking for objects that moved against the background of stars?

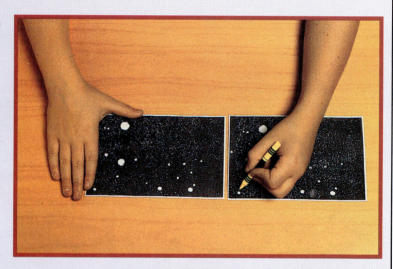

ACTIVITY

Searching for Planet X

How do you think you would feel if you discovered a new planet? In this activity, you can re-create the thrill of Clyde Tombaugh's discovery.

DO THIS

1 Look at the top left corner of the two photographic plates.

2 Use one crayon to circle the image that appears on both plates in the same position.

3 Use the same crayon to circle the other images that appear on both plates in the same positions.

4 Do you see an image that is in two different positions? If so, circle the image in both positions with your second crayon. Hurray, you have found a planet!

THINK AND WRITE

1. What is the real name of the planet you circled in different positions on the plates and that Clyde Tombaugh discovered?

2. Why was it possible to see the planet's image change position in just a few nights?

Uranus, Neptune, and Pluto

Circling the cold far reaches of our solar system are the two remaining gas planets—Uranus and Neptune—and a small, rocky planet, Pluto. Each of these planets is mysterious in its own way.

Uranus is blue-green because it has an atmosphere of methane gas. The planet has a set of dark, narrow rings. Astronomers think that its moon Miranda was broken apart by an impact but later fell back together in the strange shape it has now.

Another ringed planet, Neptune, is the bluest planet because of its methane gas atmosphere. The white clouds are methane ice. Neptune's great dark spot is a huge storm. Its moon Triton has volcanoes. Triton's strange surface has caused it to be nicknamed "the cantaloupe moon."

Pluto is the only outer planet without a thick atmosphere. Little is known about Pluto, except that it has one known moon, Charon. Charon is half the size of its planet, so Pluto and Charon are often considered a double planet. From Earth, Pluto and Charon can be seen only as small dots, even with the best telescopes.

THINK ABOUT IT

Why are Pluto and Charon sometimes called twin planets?

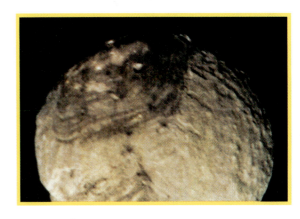

▲ Miranda

▼ Neptune and Triton

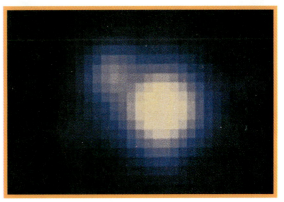

▶ Pluto and Charon

Comets Come and Comets Go

People have always marveled at the short visits of ghostly flares spread across the sky. What are these objects? Where do they come from, and where do they go?

Comets are chunks of ice and rock left over from the formation of our solar system. They are often called "dirty snowballs." They move around the sun in long, oval-shaped orbits. Comets may take from about 3 years to many millions of years to complete their orbits. Comets probably come from a large cloud of frozen chunks of material surrounding our solar system.

The strangest feature of a comet is its tail. As a comet approaches the sun, part of the comet melts and vaporizes. This causes a long, visible gas tail to stream behind the comet. Notice how the tail always points away from the sun.

In 1993 astronomers got a real treat. They photographed a comet that had been pulled apart by Jupiter's gravity. The comet's pieces have fallen into Jupiter's atmosphere.

▼ The orbits of some comets

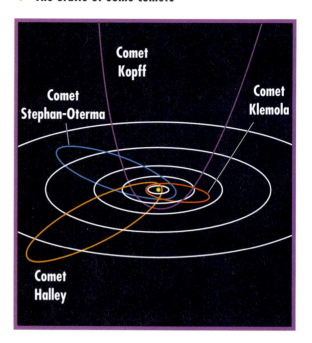

THINK ABOUT IT

Will comets orbiting around the sun last forever? Explain.

▲ A comet's tail always points away from the sun.

Showers of Meteors

Perhaps you've looked up on a star-filled night and seen a light that flashed across the sky and disappeared. You may have heard someone exclaim, "There goes a shooting star!" What are "shooting stars," and when can you see them?

In fact, shooting stars are not stars at all. They are *meteors.* And what are meteors? Let's return to the topic of comets for a moment. Comets leave behind a trail of gas and dust, or *meteoroids,* as they move through the solar system. When the Earth passes through these dust particles, they stream into our atmosphere as meteors. Because most of them are no bigger than a grain of sand, they burn up in a flash of light. Sometimes a meteor is large enough to survive its plunge and hit the surface of the Earth. Then the piece of rock is called a *meteorite.*

▲ Meteor

The Earth passes through the same paths of comet dust each year. This produces yearly showers of meteors. Sometimes you can see several meteors per hour. Other meteor showers may have hundreds of meteors per hour in a spectacular display. The table lists some major yearly meteor showers that you can watch.

METEOR SHOWERS		
Name	**Date**	**Meteors per Hour**
Quadrantids	January 3	50
Lyrids	April 22	10
Delta Aquarids	July 31	25
Perseids	August 12	50
Orionids	October 21	20
Taurids	November 8	10
Leonids	November 17	10
Geminids	December 14	50

LESSON 3 REVIEW

❶ How are most of the outer planets alike? Which one is different? Explain.

❷ During a meteor shower, why are more meteors likely to be seen between midnight and dawn than earlier in the evening?

4 WHAT'S OUT THERE?

Are we alone in the universe? Is Earth the only planet that contains intelligent life? Read this page and do the following activity to see how scientists have looked for other life in the universe.

Message to the Unknown

Some scientists say the conditions that led to life on Earth are rare. Others say there may be millions of planets with intelligent life. Here is one way to find out.

Since 1960 astronomers have been using radio telescopes to try to detect signs of other intelligent life in the universe. In 1974 American astronomer Frank Drake sent a message from Earth. The message was in code and was beamed into space by the world's biggest radio telescope, at Arecibo, Puerto Rico. The coded message is shown in the diagram. It tells any intelligent observers about Earth. In 1992 a full-scale program called *SETI* (*S*earch for *Extra*terrestrial *I*ntelligence) was begun, using radio channels all over the Earth.

Look at the information in the code. The figure shown in red stands for a human being. The solar system is shown in yellow. Why is one of the objects positioned above the others? Symbols for the numbers 1 to 10, at the top, are in white. The major chemical elements on Earth are in green. The DNA code is in blue.

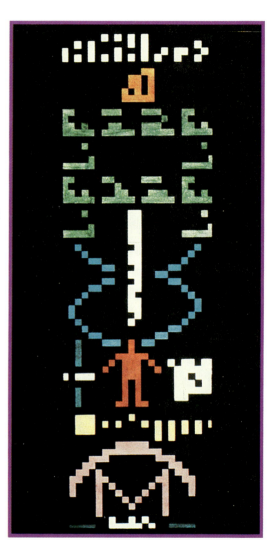

▲ SETI message

THINK ABOUT IT

How would scientists know whether a signal they receive is a message from intelligent life?

A C T I V I T Y

Contact

Suppose you are going to send a new code into space. The message will tell other life in the universe about our planet. Surprise! You receive an answer. You can communicate with an intelligent being from another planet.

MATERIALS
- colored pencils
- the SETI code
- Science Log data sheet

DO THIS

❶ Make a list of four important things about Earth that you think other intelligent beings should know.

❷ Draw a diagram that shows these things in some way. Use the SETI diagram for ideas.

❸ Color your coded message. At the bottom, show what each symbol in your diagram stands for. Have a classmate try to decode your message.

❹ Draw a picture of what you think the extraterrestrial being would look like.

THINK AND WRITE

Explain why you pictured the extraterrestrial being as you did.

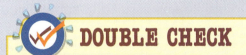

LESSON 4 REVIEW

What are several problems with the SETI approach to the search for other intelligent life in the universe?

DOUBLE CHECK

SECTION B REVIEW

1. Explain how Earth is more like the other inner planets than the outer planets.

2. Explain how astronomers can predict and find previously unknown planets in our solar system.

SECTION C
Stars Above

Have you ever joined others on a clear night for a stargazing party? If not, then try it sometime. It's fun! You can bring a star chart, a pair of binoculars or a telescope, or just your own two eyes and your wondering mind. Whether you enjoy finding patterns of stars or using different kinds of telescopes, this section will help make your stargazing activities a success. You will also explore some possible answers to questions you may have asked about the universe.

What stars appear above the eastern horizon soon after sunset? Do they change? Do some stars seem to be grouped together in a pattern? What star groupings do you recognize? Work through the following investigations. In your Science Log, answer the above questions and describe some of your night-sky observations.

THE CELESTIAL SHOW

On any clear night, gaze upward and you can view a sky show. Against a domelike background, patterns of stars march across the sky. You will meet some of the "actors" as they give their stellar performances.

Stars on Stage

Let's set the stage for the nightly parade of stars across the sky. Astronomers use the following model to locate and track stars and planets.

Think of stars as being attached to the inside of a large hollow sphere surrounding the smaller sphere that is the Earth. This imaginary sphere of sky is called the *celestial sphere.* From any point on Earth, you can see only half of the celestial sphere. That half appears as if it meets the Earth at the horizon. In the diagram, you can see the axis, the poles, and the equator of the celestial sphere. They are extensions of the axis, the poles, and the equator of the Earth.

Observe a clear night sky for several hours and you will notice that stars appear to rise above the eastern part of the horizon and set below the western part of the horizon. For convenience, astronomers think of the celestial sphere as rotating. Actually, this is not so. Since the Earth rotates from west to east, the celestial sphere seems to rotate from east to west. One complete rotation takes 23 hours 56 minutes 4.09 seconds—slightly less than a 24-hour day.

▼ **Celestial sphere**

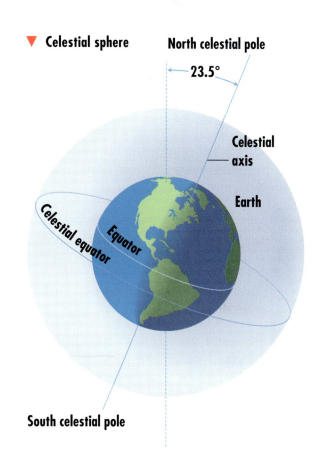

North celestial pole

23.5°

Celestial axis

Earth

Celestial equator

Equator

South celestial pole

THINK ABOUT IT

On a certain night at 9:00 P.M., a bright star appears on the horizon. If that star is viewed at 9:00 P.M. on each night during a year, how will its position change?

Pictures in the Night Sky

Ancient observers noticed that stars seemed to be arranged in groups, or *constellations.* These constellations were pictured as figures in the sky. For example, Orion was the great hunter, and Cassiopeia (kas ee oh PEE uh) was the queen on her throne. You can make and project some of these constellations for yourself and others to view.

DO THIS

1. On your paper, draw around the box's bottom.

2. Choose a constellation, and mark its star pattern heavily in the circle on the paper.

3. Lay the star pattern face up on top of the sealed end of the box.

4. Use a pencil to punch a hole in the bottom of the box for each star.

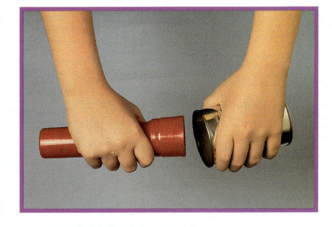

5. Put the lighted flashlight inside the box, and show your constellation on a wall in a darkened room.

THINK AND WRITE

1. Draw and identify each classmate's constellation. Do research and write a paragraph about the mythology of each constellation.

2. **FORMULATING AND USING MODELS** When making models, you should read through all the steps and gather all the materials you need before you begin. Why do you think you drew the shape of the constellation and placed it on the box before punching holes in the box? What other uses can you think of for your class's constellation projectors?

Finding the North Star

In the last activity, you made a model of a constellation. In this activity, you can use two stars of a well-known constellation to point you to the star closest to the celestial north pole.

DO THIS

1 Find the constellation Ursa Major, which contains the stars known as the Big Dipper, on the star chart.

2 Locate the two stars on the front edge of the Dipper's cup.

3 Line up your ruler along these stars, and then follow the line north until you reach a star.

THINK AND WRITE

1. Which star did you find along the ruler's line?

2. How can you show that this star is indeed the star that is closest to the north celestial pole of the celestial sphere?

Circumpolar stars At the latitude of your location, some stars appear to rise and set just like the sun. Others, called *circumpolar* ("around the pole") *stars*, are always above the horizon. The star you located, Polaris, is the north pole star since it is the star closest to the north celestial pole of the celestial sphere.

The north pole star always appears directly above the Earth's North Pole. Its height above the horizon is the same as the latitude of your location.

The Sun's Parade

Did you know that the sun passes through various constellations on the celestial sphere? How could you identify these constellations? In this activity, you will model the Earth's movement around the sun.

DO THIS

1. Draw a constellation pattern on a sheet of poster board for two of the following constellations: Aquarius, Pisces, Aries, Taurus, Gemini, Cancer, Leo, Virgo, Libra, Scorpius, Sagittarius, Capricornus.

2. Clear a large space, and set up the desk with the lighted lamp (sun) on top.

3. Twelve classmates should hold different posters in a circle, facing the sun in the center. They should stand in the order given in step 1, from Aquarius to Capricornus.

4. Other classmates should take turns being the Earth and revolving slowly around the sun, staying between the lamp and the constellations. They should notice both the constellations they face and those behind the sun.

THINK AND WRITE

1. Suppose that while looking away from the sun, you face the constellation Taurus. In which constellation does the sun appear?

2. If you cannot see the sun's position in a constellation because of the sun's light, how can you tell which constellation it is in?

Circle of Animals

In the last activity, you modeled the Earth's revolution around the sun and noted the sun's location in some constellations. Here is how the Earth's revolution is shown on the celestial sphere.

Throughout the year, as the Earth orbits the sun, observers see different constellations in the night sky. Ancient people noted that the sun appeared to move through the same star patterns year after year. They named this path the *ecliptic.* The ecliptic is an imaginary circle on the celestial sphere. It represents the changing position of the sun against the background of stars, as seen from the Earth.

The 12 constellations that lie in the ecliptic's path are called the *zodiac.* This comes from a Greek word that means "circle of animals." Can you see why?

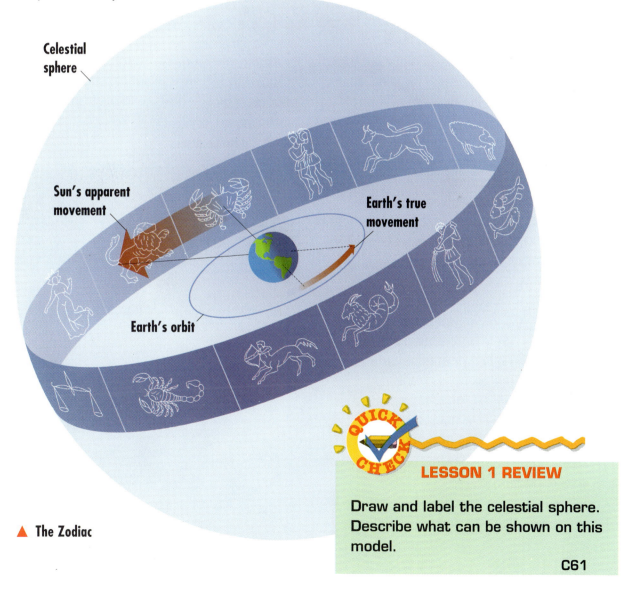

Celestial sphere

Sun's apparent movement

Earth's true movement

Earth's orbit

▲ The Zodiac

2 EYES ON THE SKY

Since the early 1600s, people have had tools to help them view the universe. In this lesson, you can find out about the telescopes that can help you get a better look at the universe.

Starry-Eyed

Read about a group of students who learned firsthand about telescopes.

Seeing Stars

by **Judith E. Rinard**
from *National Geographic World*

LITERATURE

"It was so exciting to see the planets!" says Christina Vitale, 12, a Junior Member from Tucson, Arizona. "My favorite was Saturn. It's just beautiful. We could see its moons and rings. All the rings looked like a rainbow of orange and other colors." Last summer Christina viewed the planets, stars, and galaxies through powerful telescopes when she attended the University of Arizona Alumni Association's Astronomy Camp in Tucson.

The camp session lasted one week. The student astronomers spent the first three days at the university. They toured nearby Flandrau Planetarium and Kitt Peak Observatory. Going behind the scenes, they examined huge telescopes. At the university's mirror lab, they watched as scientists made some of the world's biggest telescope mirrors.

Each evening the campers learned about the night sky and constellations from professional astronomers. They listened to lectures on space, stars, and comets by scientists, experts from NASA, and space artists.

▼ **Telescope domes**

◀ **Marian Toro launches her rocket. "I couldn't believe it flew so well."**

During the day the campers split up into research teams to do experiments. They investigated planet temperatures, tracked satellites, and built small telescopes and model rockets. Campers came from many different places. One of them, Marian Toro, 17, came from Sells, Arizona. She is a Native American of the Tohono O'odham Nation, once called the Papago. She lives on the reservation, 60 miles west of Tucson.

"I'm really interested in astronomy," says Marian. "Kitt Peak is right on our reservation. It is part of a mountain range that is sacred to us. Our people have always believed that our creator stays in a cave there but dwells throughout the mountains. Long ago, our people looked at the moon and stars to tell if crops would be good. Now people study the stars with telescopes."

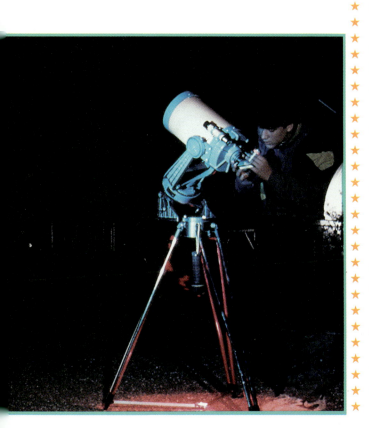

The highlight of the week was spending four days and nights using telescopes at the observatory on Mount Lemmon. The telescopes, used by research astronomers, are stationed on the mountaintop, 9,200 feet high.

Through the observatory's open domes, teams used the 40-inch and 60-inch telescopes to observe objects in the night sky. The camp counselors, who were graduate students in astronomy, taught them how to position the huge telescopes to view each object.

"We stayed up until three every morning," says Marian. "I saw Jupiter and its Red Spot. The Ring Nebula, a ring of colored gases, was beautiful."

By the end of the week the campers had great souvenirs—photographs of the night sky they took through special cameras attached to the telescopes. Some of the campers began thinking of careers as astronomers.

"I really enjoyed camp," says Chris Cadle. "It's a neat experience to go to the top of a mountain to see what's out there."

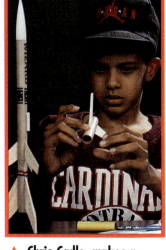

▲ **Chris Cadle makes a model rocket.**

THINK ABOUT IT

Why are many telescopes located on mountaintops?

Catching the Light

Telescopes, like those used by the students at the astronomy camp, gather and focus light. They make distant objects look brighter, clearer, and larger. Read about the invention of two kinds of telescopes used today.

In 1609, Italian scientist Galileo Galilei was the first scientist to use a telescope for astronomy. However, he did not invent it. A Dutch eyeglass maker named Hans Lippershey was looking through different pairs of lenses one day. Suddenly he saw distant objects spring into view as if they were close up. Lippershey had accidentally invented the telescope!

The Lippershey-Galileo telescope is a *refracting* telescope. It uses two glass lenses to refract, or bend, light and focus it to form an image. The objective lens gathers the light. The eyepiece lens magnifies the image. The larger the objective lens, the brighter and clearer the image. Galileo's objective lens was only 26 mil-limeters (1.01 inches) in diameter. Yet it opened up a universe of previously unseen stars to astronomers.

About 60 years later, Isaac Newton invented a *reflecting* telescope. He used mirrors instead of glass lenses to gather and focus light. Newton's objective mirror was only 2.5 centimeters (about 1 inch) in diameter.

THINK ABOUT IT

Why do you think reflecting telescopes with larger and larger objective mirrors are built?

▼ Galileo with his telescope

▲ Sir Isaac Newton

A C T I V I T Y

The Refracting Telescope

You can repeat Hans Lippershey's accidental discovery of the refracting telescope. Complete this activity to see for yourself how a refracting telescope works.

MATERIALS
- **2 convex lenses**
- **Science Log data sheet**

DO THIS

❶ **CAUTION: Never use lenses to look at the sun.** Hold up one lens of the pair, and look through it at a distant object.

❷ Move the lens back and forth until the image is clear.

❸ Keep the first lens in the same position. Then hold the second lens near your eye. Move it back and forth in line with the first lens until you again see a clear image of the object.

THINK AND WRITE

1. When you completed step 2, how did the object appear?

2. When you completed step 3, how did the object appear?

ACTIVITY

The Reflecting Telescope

Newton reasoned that a certain type of mirror could do the same things as a lens. Complete this activity to discover how a reflecting telescope works.

MATERIALS
- candle in holder
- safety matches
- concave mirror
- table
- hand lens
- Science Log data sheet

DO THIS

1. **CAUTION: Be careful near the flame.** Your teacher will light the candle and place it at one end of the table.

2. Place the mirror at the opposite end of the table.

3. Move the mirror until it reflects the image of the candle onto the wall.

4. Use the magnifying glass to make the candle image larger.

THINK AND WRITE

1. Describe in your own words how a reflecting telescope works.

2. What advantage does a reflecting telescope with a larger diameter mirror have over one with a smaller mirror?

Skylight!

Most of the telescopes that astronomers use to observe the universe are located on Earth. However, some are located in space. Space-based telescopes allow astronomers to look deeper into the universe. Read about three large telescopes, and find out what makes each one useful.

The largest refracting telescope, with a 1-meter (40-inch) diameter objective lens, is at Yerkes Observatory in Williams Bay, Wisconsin. The telescope was completed in 1897. Since then it has been used to study the planets and to measure star positions and movements. The Yerkes telescope is likely to remain the largest refracting telescope. Glass is heavy and larger lenses would bend, distorting the view.

▲ The Yerkes refractor is often used to track stars and planets.

Reflecting telescopes can be much larger, because mirrors can be made of lightweight material. The Keck I telescope sits at an altitude of 4,205 meters (13,796 feet) on the top of Mauna Kea volcano on

▼ Keck telescope

Hawai'i. It is the largest reflecting telescope in the world. Its main mirror measures 10 meters (33 feet) in diameter. This mirror is made up of 36 smaller hexagonal mirrors. Each smaller mirror's position is controlled by a computer system. As a result, the mirror, as a whole, will focus light properly. Large reflecting telescopes like the Keck I are mostly used to study quasars and faint galaxies.

Mountaintops offer the best views from Earth. But astronomers have long wanted to put a telescope above the Earth's atmosphere and pollution. In April 1990, the space shuttle *Discovery* placed the Hubble Space Telescope into orbit.

At first, the Hubble Space Telescope did not work as expected. In December 1993, the crew of the space shuttle *Endeavour* made repairs on the telescope. It is now sending back clearer pictures.

Here is what a clear picture means. Think of how a distant car's headlights look as they approach you. At first, the two headlights are a blur, and then, as they get closer, they separate into two distinct lights. The Hubble Space Telescope can separate images of very faint distant stars that are close together better than other telescopes.

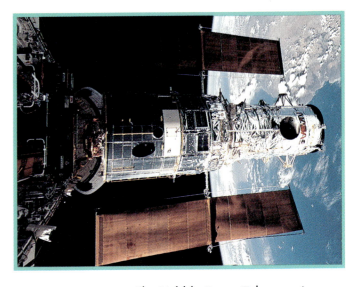

▲ The Hubble Space Telescope is the size of a school bus. Its objective mirror is 2.4 meters (almost 8 feet) in diameter.

▲ The Hubble Space Telescope's shot of Pluto and its moon Charon (left) is much more distinct than an Earth-based photograph (right).

LESSON 2 REVIEW

Explain in your own words how refracting and reflecting telescopes work. Make a chart to list their similarities and differences.

3 ISLANDS IN THE UNIVERSE

As astronomers on StarBase Earth look deeper into space, they find more and more giant groups of stars rushing away from each other. Where are these star groups going?

The Backbone of Night

A mysterious faint glow in the sky inspired many myths among ancient people. How did the ancients describe this glow?

◀ The star-filled Milky Way Galaxy led to fanciful myths and stories.

Maybe you have seen this softly glowing ribbon of light stretching across the sky. To some ancient Greeks, it looked like a river of milk. So they called it the *Milky Way.*

Ancient people of Botswana, in Africa, saw a different picture. They saw what appeared to be a structure holding up the sky. They called it the *Backbone of Night.*

The ancient Greek thinkers Pythagoras and Democritus hypothesized that the ribbon of light is really a ribbon of stars.

Hundreds of years later, Galileo viewed these stars through his telescope.

Our solar system, the ribbon of stars, and all other stars in the sky form one large group, or *galaxy.* Millions of galaxies spread out like islands in a sea of space. Astronomers still call our galaxy the *Milky Way Galaxy.*

THINK ABOUT IT

How did Pythagoras and Democritus use scientific thinking?

ACTIVITY

It Depends on Your Viewpoint!

The ribbon of stars and the shape of our Milky Way Galaxy suggest the location of our solar system. Based on what you know, where do you think our solar system is located? Now, test your hypothesis.

MATERIALS
- paper to be recycled
- low, flat table
- drawing paper
- Science Log data sheet

DO THIS

1. Make dozens of "stars" by wadding scrap paper into balls.

2. Arrange the paper stars on the table-top in the shape of a spiral, as shown in the diagram. Pile more stars on top of each other in the center, and put fewer along the spiral arms.

3. Look directly across the surface of the table through the paper stars. Draw what you see.

4. Then, look down on the paper stars. Draw what you see.

THINK AND WRITE

1. Compare the pictures you drew in steps 3 and 4 with the diagrams on this page and on page C71. Which drawing is more like this diagram? Which is more like the one on page C71?

2. Where do you now think our solar system is located in our galaxy?

3. **HYPOTHESIZING** A hypothesis is an explanation based on what you already know. In this activity, you formulated and tested a hypothesis. How did your actions test your hypothesis?

▲ Spiral Galaxy

Space in Space

Remember the AU—the unit you used to mark distances in the solar system? Distances beyond the solar system are much greater. Read the following to find out how much greater.

Astronomers do not use kilometers or astronomical units to measure these greater distances. The numbers would be far too large. Instead, they measure distances in *light-years*. A light-year is the distance light travels in a year. With a speed of about 300,000 kilometers (186,000 miles) per second, light travels about 10 trillion kilometers (6 trillion miles) in a year.

Our Milky Way Galaxy contains up to 200 billion stars. The galaxy extends 100,000 light-years from edge to edge. The center is about 10,000 light-years wide. The sun and Earth are about 30,000 light-years from the center of the galaxy, as shown in the diagram.

▼ **Milky Way Galaxy**

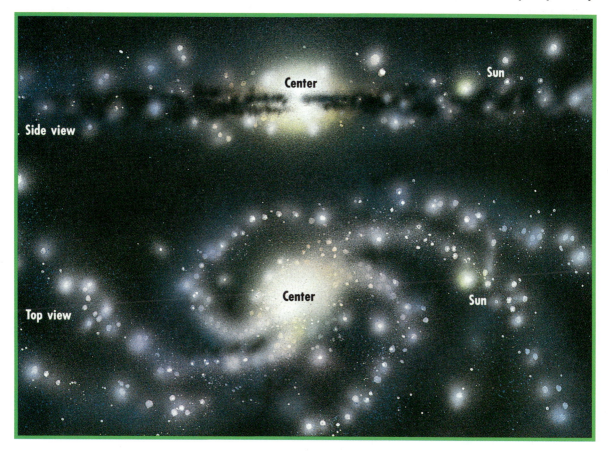

Side view
Center
Sun

Top view
Center
Sun

This means that we cannot travel across the galaxy, or even a short way through it. Voyager, traveling much slower than the speed of light, took 12 years to reach Neptune. That distance is only a small fraction of the distance in a light-year.

Telescopes have enabled people on StarBase Earth to locate stars in our own galaxy and to determine its shape. Telescopes can also show astronomers the size and the beauty of other galaxies.

▼ Galaxy M87 has an elliptical shape and contains a thousand billion old red stars.

▼ Galaxy M104 is nicknamed the Sombrero Galaxy because, when seen through a telescope, it looks like a hat. It is 40 million light-years away.

▲ The Andromeda Galaxy is a spiral galaxy like the Milky Way Galaxy. It is one of only three galaxies that can be seen from Earth without a telescope. It is only 2.3 million light-years away.

THINK ABOUT IT

Suppose you could visit a planet like Earth somewhere in each of the galaxies shown. How might the night sky appear from each planet?

Beginnings and Endings

How did the universe begin? Will it ever end? You can act out two theories that astronomers have developed to answer these questions.

▲ Galaxies and clusters of galaxies all speed away from each other as the universe expands.

Many scientists think that about 15 billion years ago, all the matter in the universe was squeezed into a tiny, hot point. Then, in an instant, this matter began to expand outward in all directions, as if a giant explosion had occurred. The matter cooled and clumped together, forming galaxies. Today, the universe is still expanding. The amount of matter and its gravitational attraction will determine whether the expansion continues or stops. Let's act out two possible futures.

On an open field, stand with some of your classmates in a tight circle, facing outward. Other classmates should stand far away from the circle and should observe what happens. You and the others in the circle should begin to walk straight outward until told to stop. Then turn around and look at everyone else's position. Turn to face the center of the circle and walk inward. When you rejoin the others in a tight circle, stop and face outward again. Now use the theories and your observations to answer the following questions.

What will happen to the galaxies of the universe if the universe continues to expand forever?

What will happen to the galaxies of the universe if gravity stops the expansion and causes them to return to the point where they started?

LESSON 3 REVIEW

1 How do you know that the sun is located within a spiral arm of our galaxy?

2 How do some scientists explain how the universe began and what its future might be?

DOUBLE CHECK

SECTION C REVIEW

1. Which stars in the northern hemisphere do not seem to rise and set in the sky? Explain.

2. Why is the Hubble telescope in space able to take better pictures of space objects than the Yerkes telescope in Wisconsin?

SECTION D
Stars Near and Far

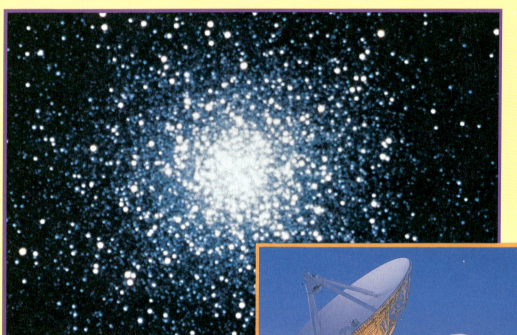

▲ Radio telescopes

Do you ever try to count the stars you see in the night sky? If you do, you will count some bright stars and many more faint stars. Like our star, the sun, the stars you see from StarBase Earth and many billions of fainter stars are all powerful sources of heat and light. This section discusses the kinds of energy that stars produce, why some stars are brighter than others, and how stars are born, age, and burn out.

On a clear night, observe the brighter stars in the sky. What is the color of each bright star? Use a star chart to identify these stars by name. In your Science Log, list each of these and its color. As you work through the following investigations, research the stars in your list. For each one, write three things that you find out.

1 ▼ HOME STAR

For about 5 billion years, StarBase Earth has been bathed in the sun's heat and light. An environment has slowly developed in which plants and animals, including humans, can thrive. In this lesson, you will find out what the sun is really like and how it provides the Earth with energy.

Our Sun's Different Looks

StarBase Earth's star, the sun, has been photographed by both Earth-based and orbiting telescopes. Some pictures, taken by regular cameras using visible light, show what we can see with our eyes. Other pictures show a very different kind of sun. See for yourself!

▼ This is a visible-light photograph of sunspots on the sun's surface.

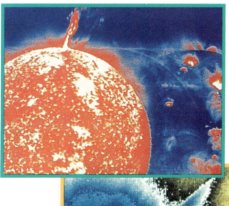

◄ This photograph, taken by *Skylab,* shows a *solar prominence.* It's a huge cloud of burning gas that blasts out from the sun's surface.

◄ This *Skylab* coronagraph was taken by blocking out the sun's surface in order to see the corona, the sun's outer atmosphere.

▲ A radio telescope and a computer made this map of the sun's radio-wave activity. The red spots are clouds of hot gas. They would show up as sunspots in a visible-light photograph.

THINK ABOUT IT

Describe two characteristics of the sun that show it is not a perfectly smooth ball of light.

What's Going On in There?

As you have seen, our sun is much more active than it appears to be. Let's look inside the sun and see how it produces all that energy.

The sun is about 1.4 million kilometers (870,000 miles) in diameter, about 100 times the diameter of the Earth. It is large enough to hold one million Earths. Like all stars, the sun is a large globe of hot gas.

Photosphere
The photosphere, or "sphere of light," is the part of the sun that we see. The sun's energy is given off here, at the surface. The surface temperature is about 5,500 degrees Celsius. At this temperature, the light given off appears to us as yellowish white or orange.

Radiative Layer
This area is warmed by the core and in turn, warms the next layer. The temperature is about 3 million degrees Celsius.

Convective Layer
The energy is moved through this layer the same way it is moved by gas bubbles to the surface of boiling water. The temperature here is about 1.1 million degrees Celsius.

Core
The hydrogen gas at the core of the sun is compressed and heated by the weight of the outer layers. At a temperature of about 15 million degrees Celsius, the hydrogen atoms combine to make helium. The energy produced by this nuclear reaction radiates outward to heat the sun's gaseous outer layers. Only gravity keeps the sun from blowing apart.

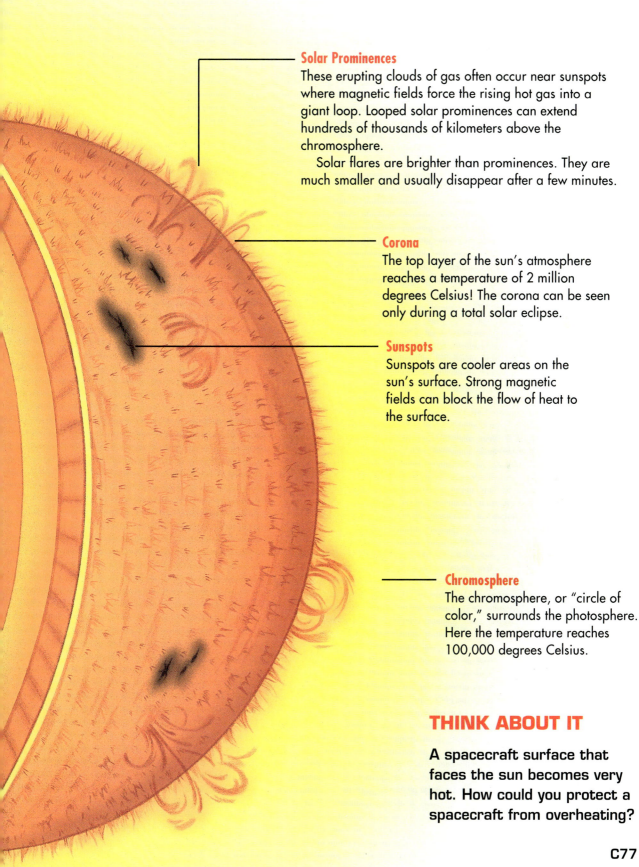

Solar Prominences

These erupting clouds of gas often occur near sunspots where magnetic fields force the rising hot gas into a giant loop. Looped solar prominences can extend hundreds of thousands of kilometers above the chromosphere.

Solar flares are brighter than prominences. They are much smaller and usually disappear after a few minutes.

Corona

The top layer of the sun's atmosphere reaches a temperature of 2 million degrees Celsius! The corona can be seen only during a total solar eclipse.

Sunspots

Sunspots are cooler areas on the sun's surface. Strong magnetic fields can block the flow of heat to the surface.

Chromosphere

The chromosphere, or "circle of color," surrounds the photosphere. Here the temperature reaches 100,000 degrees Celsius.

THINK ABOUT IT

A spacecraft surface that faces the sun becomes very hot. How could you protect a spacecraft from overheating?

ACTIVITY

X Marks the Spot!

You've learned what makes up the sun and its layers. By observing sunspots, you can find out something very important about what the sun does.

DO THIS

1 **CAUTION: Never look directly at the sun with your eyes alone or through an eyepiece. You could be permanently blinded!** Point the telescope so that a magnified image of the sun shows through the eyepiece and onto the paper or cardboard.

2 If you use binoculars, block one eyepiece with the small piece of cardboard and tape.

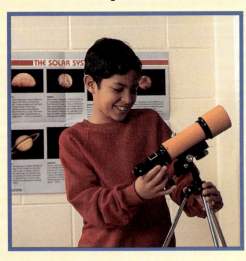

3 Note the sunspots that appear on the white paper or cardboard.

4 Lay the tracing paper over the cardboard, and trace the outline of the sun. Record the positions of the sunspots over several days.

5 About one month later, record the positions of the sunspots again.

MATERIALS

- small telescope, or binoculars with supporting stand
- large sheet of white paper or cardboard
- small piece of cardboard
- tape
- sheet of thin tracing paper
- Science Log data sheet

THINK AND WRITE

1. What can you conclude about the positions of the sunspots over several days?

2. When observing the sun's surface one month later, did you see any of the sunspots that you had observed before?

3. What can you conclude about the sun's movement, based on your responses to questions 1 and 2? Explain.

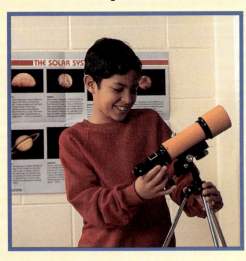

The Sun's Bubble

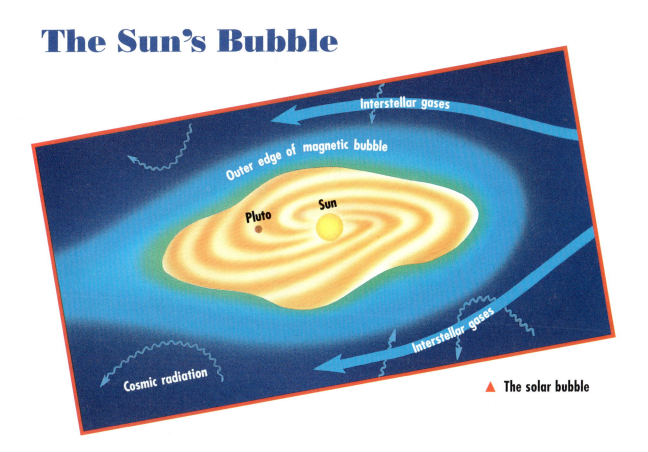

Interstellar gases

Outer edge of magnetic bubble

Pluto   Sun

Interstellar gases

Cosmic radiation

▲ The solar bubble

You probably wouldn't think that it's windy out there in our solar system, but it is. Surprised? Read to find out what the sun blows through the solar system.

It doesn't seem to make sense that there could be a wind in space. After all, space is empty, isn't it? Not really! The sun's corona gives off fast-moving gas that becomes the *solar wind*. The solar wind is a gale of charged atomic particles. These particles race away from the sun at speeds of up to 3 million kilometers (1.9 million miles) per hour. They generate electric currents and magnetic fields that fill the space in our solar system. The currents flow in a great, thin sheet that ripples as the sun rotates. The magnetic fields form a huge bubble

around our solar system. This bubble protects all nine planets from the cosmic radiation that exists in the space between the stars. The cosmic radiation would be harmful to life on Earth. Within the protective bubble are gases that are very hot. However, the gases are spread so thin that people on Earth and astronauts in space do not burn up.

QUICK CHECK

LESSON 1 REVIEW

Describe in your own words how the sun produces heat and light.

2 STAR LIGHT, STAR BRIGHT

Almost all stars give off blindingly bright light, but only our sun appears very bright to us. Some stars appear to be brighter than others. Why is this? How do we rank stars by their brightness? In this lesson, you will explore and answer these questions and others.

ACTIVITY

Burning Bright!

What causes some stars to look so bright and others to look so dim? This activity will help you test your hypothesis.

MATERIALS
- 2 lamps
- bulbs of various wattages: 40, 60
- darkened corridor or room
- Science Log data sheet

DO THIS

❶ Place two lighted lamps, one with a 40-watt and the other with a 60-watt bulb, halfway down the corridor. Observe both from the corridor's end.

❷ Move the lamp with the 60-watt bulb to the far end of the corridor. Again, observe both from the opposite end of the corridor.

❸ Observe bulbs of different wattages at a variety of distances.

THINK AND WRITE

1. In step 1, which lamp was brighter? How did step 2 change the apparent brightness of the two lamps?

2. What other observations did you make with bulbs of different wattages at different distances?

3. Based on your observations, what two factors affect the brightness of stars as they appear to us?

4. **EXPERIMENTING** A hypothesis should be tested by an experiment. How completely did this experiment test your hypothesis?

From Bright to Dim

Today's astronomers use an ancient way of comparing the brightness of stars. You can use this method to find the brightness of any star that you see.

You have probably seen the stars Betelgeuse and Rigel in the night sky. Betelgeuse is one of the largest stars known. Betelgeuse and Rigel are in the constellation Orion. Both stars are very bright. In fact, they are among the brightest stars in the night sky.

Orion

Astronomers use the word *magnitude* to refer to a star's brightness. *Apparent magnitude* refers to how bright a star appears to us. Apparent magnitude is based on how much light a star gives off and how far away from Earth the star is.

Over 2,000 years ago, the Greek astronomer Hipparchus (hih PAHR kuhs) classified stars that were visible to the unaided eye into six magnitudes. Magnitude 6 stars were the dimmest. Magnitude 1 stars were the brightest. This scale has been extended to include brighter and fainter stars. Rigel has an apparent magnitude of 0, brighter even than Betelgeuse, a magnitude 1 star. Sirius—the brightest star—has an apparent magnitude of –1.5. Today, with very large telescopes, we can see stars as dim as magnitude 25.

The measure of a star's actual brightness is its *absolute magnitude*. Let's look again at Sirius and Rigel. Which star is really brighter? In terms of absolute magnitude, Rigel is magnitude –6. Sirius has an absolute magnitude of only 1.4. Sirius appears to be brighter because it is much closer to Earth. It is only 9 light-years away (the distance light travels through space in 9 years), while Rigel is 815 light-years away!

▼ This star chart of the midevening winter sky shows some of the brighter stars and their apparent magnitudes. Find Betelgeuse, Rigel, and Sirius. The chart shows that they are among the brightest of stars.

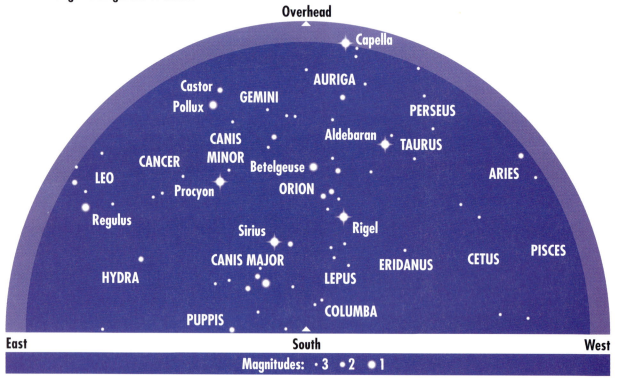

THINK ABOUT IT

Look at the star chart above. What other stars can you find that have very bright apparent magnitudes? Which constellations are these stars in?

Let's Get Warmed Up!

Visible light is just a small part of the energy given off by stars. Another form is infrared radiation, or heat.

We detect light with our eyes. Our bodies detect infrared radiation as heat. An infrared photograph can be used to identify heat sources. White and yellow represent the hottest areas. Blue and green represent the coolest. Astronomers gain useful information about planets, stars, and galaxies from infrared photographs.

Look at the photograph below. Which part shows the most heat? What do you think the man is holding that is so hot? Notice the man's hand and face. Why are they different? How do you explain this?

THINK ABOUT IT

How might an infrared photograph of the Earth be useful to scientists?

▼ Infrared photo

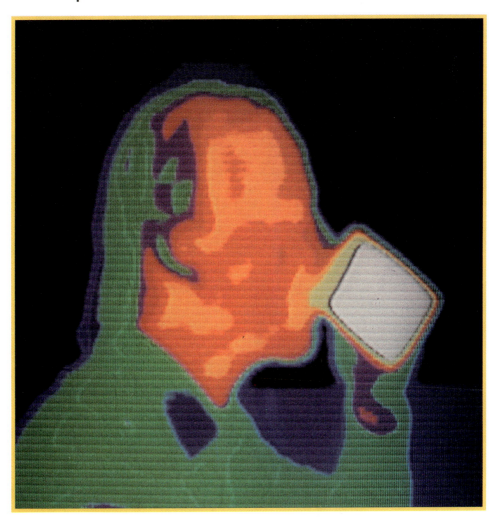

Riding the Waves!

Stars give off a wide range of energy. You have explored two forms of this energy—light and heat. The diagram shows other forms of energy that astronomers measure and record.

▼ Gamma rays are used to preserve foods at less cost than canning or freezing methods.

▼ X-rays are used to take pictures of the inside of the body.

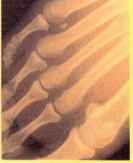

▼ Ultraviolet waves from the sun can burn your skin. Sunscreen lotion protects you from these waves.

▼ Ordinary photographs show the same things that our eyes see in visible light.

Gamma rays	X-rays	Ultraviolet waves	Visible-light waves

▲ Gamma rays come from very energetic objects in space.

▲ X-rays in space come from areas around stars and from exploding stars.

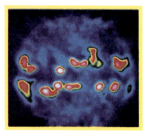

▲ Ultraviolet waves given off by young stars in a cloud of gas make the gas glow magenta.

▲ A visible-light photograph of a star cluster shows thousands of tightly grouped stars.

Visible light represents only a small part of this energy. Visible light divides into colors when it passes through a prism, a wet atmosphere, or a soap bubble. What are the colors?

All energy travels through space as waves. The waves all travel at the speed of light. But some waves are very long, and some are very short. All these forms of energy can be produced on Earth artificially.

▼ **Infrared waves are felt by our bodies as heat.**

▼ **Microwaves can be used to cook food.**

▼ **A radar system bounces radio signals off a target and back to the receiver. The radar echo is displayed as an image on a screen.**

▼ **This radio map shows the intense radio waves coming from the center of a galaxy.**

   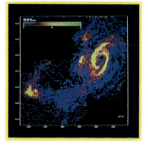

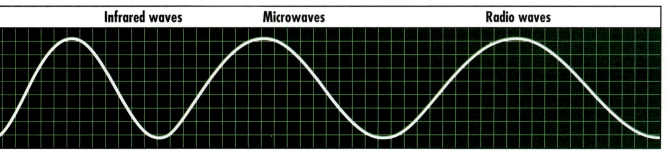

Infrared waves	Microwaves	Radio waves

 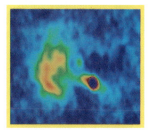

▲ **This picture of the center of the Milky Way Galaxy was made by an infrared instrument.**

▲ **This is a microwave picture of the radiation left over from the beginning of the universe.**

LESSON 2 REVIEW

Does a star's apparent magnitude tell everything about how bright the star is? Explain.

3 "LIVES" OF THE STARS

Stars come in many different sizes, temperatures, and colors.
As you will see, different stars often lead very different "lives."

You're Not in My Class!

The absolute magnitude of a star is determined by its size, mass, color, and temperature. The diagram below shows you how scientists classify stars according to their properties.

Study the diagram on page C87. Note that temperature readings are along the bottom and absolute magnitude readings are at the left.

The *main sequence* is a group of stars that lie along the curved line running from the top left to the bottom right. Many stars, including the sun, lie on this sequence.

From top to bottom, the stars go from hottest to coolest and from largest to smallest. So, in the main sequence, a large size or mass and a hot temperature mean a high absolute magnitude.

Notice that the diagram also shows stars that lie outside the main sequence. Betelgeuse (BET uhl jooz), in the constellation Orion, is a red star. If it were of an average size and mass, it would not be very bright. But Betelgeuse is a super giant—it's huge! Its size makes up for its low temperature. So Betelgeuse has a very high absolute magnitude. Stars that lie below the main sequence are very small stars. They are usually white or red. Use the diagram to answer these questions.

▼ Observatory

1. Where is the sun in the diagram? What color is it? What is its temperature? Is it a large, a medium, or a small star?

2. The sun is so close to us that its apparent magnitude is –27! What is its absolute magnitude?

3. Which other star on the diagram is much like the sun?

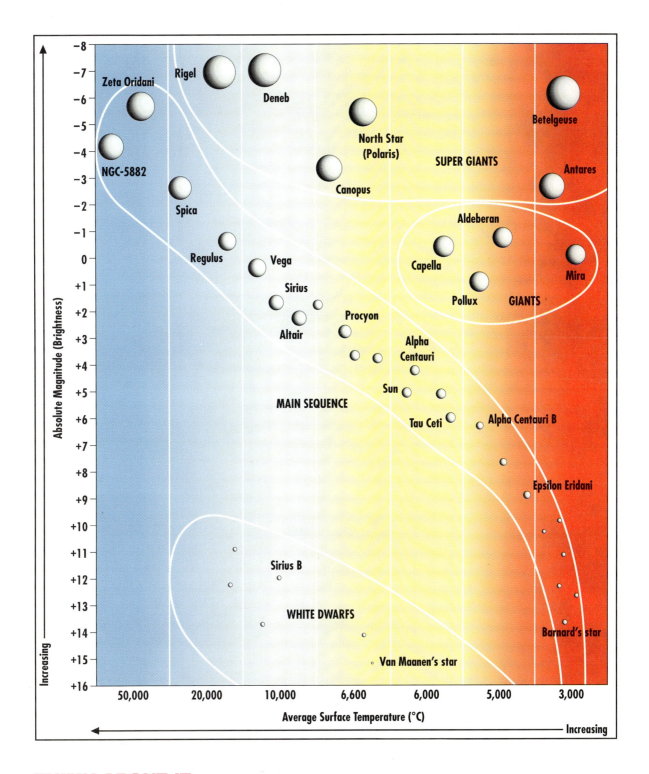

THINK ABOUT IT

What does knowing the absolute magnitude of a star tell you about that star?

Once and Future Stars

Stars have different life spans, just as Earth's creatures do. Follow the life cycles of the two stars here.

Blue star
A blue star is hotter and brighter than a yellow star.

Supergiant
The blue star becomes a supergiant that burns fuel quickly.

Supernova
A supergiant may explode into a supernova.

Neutron star
After the explosion, the star's core may shrink and become a neutron star.

New star forms

New star forms

Yellow star
A yellow star, like our sun, is a relatively small and cool star.

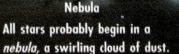

Nebula
All stars probably begin in a *nebula*, a swirling cloud of dust.

Red giant
As a yellow star uses its fuel, it begins to grow larger. It becomes a red giant, and its surface temperature drops.

Black dwarf
When the white dwarf stops giving off light, it becomes a black dwarf, just a black cinder.

White dwarf
When its outer layer blows off, the star shrinks and becomes a white dwarf. It shines with very bright white light.

QUICK CHECK

LESSON 3 REVIEW

Our sun will become a red giant, but it will never become a supernova. Explain.

DOUBLE CHECK

SECTION D REVIEW

Our sun and Capella are both yellow stars. The sun's absolute magnitude is 4.8; Capella's absolute magnitude is 0.4. Compare the sun and Capella. How will their lives differ?

Black hole

If the core shrinks to a point, it becomes a black hole. Not even light can escape a black hole's gravity.

C89

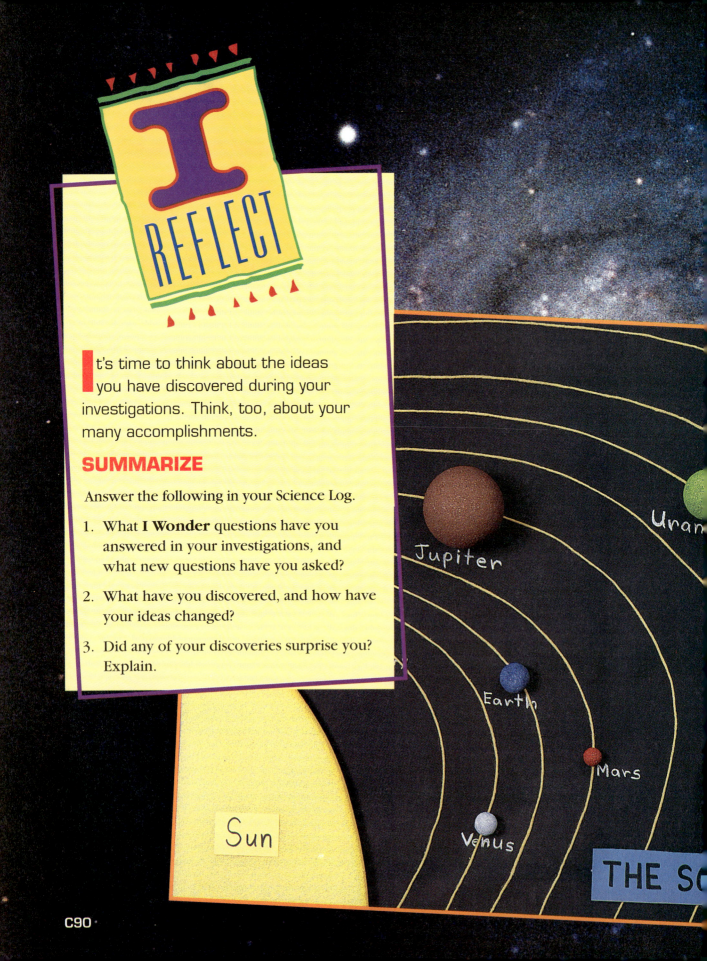

I REFLECT

It's time to think about the ideas you have discovered during your investigations. Think, too, about your many accomplishments.

SUMMARIZE

Answer the following in your Science Log.

1. What **I Wonder** questions have you answered in your investigations, and what new questions have you asked?

2. What have you discovered, and how have your ideas changed?

3. Did any of your discoveries surprise you? Explain.

Jupiter

Uran

Earth

Mars

Venus

Sun

THE SC

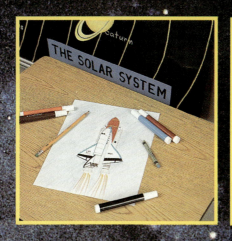

Pluto

Saturn

AR SYSTEM

CONNECT IDEAS

1. How have observations of the movements of the Earth, the moon, and the sun been used for keeping time in days, months, and years?

2. How are stars different from planets?

3. How has technology helped us increase our knowledge of the universe?

4. How do the moon and the sun affect the tides?

5. Compare the inner planets and the outer planets, and explain how the Earth differs from all other planets.

SCIENCE PORTFOLIO

1. Complete your Science Experiences Record.

2. Choose one or two samples of your best work from each section to include in your Science Portfolio.

3. On A Guide to My Science Portfolio, tell why you chose each sample.

I SHARE

Scientists share their discoveries and ideas and learn from one another. How can you share what you've learned?

Decide

▶ what you want to say.

▶ what the best way is to get your message across.

Share

▶ what you did and why.

▶ what worked and what didn't work.

▶ what conclusions you have drawn.

▶ what else you'd like to find out.

Find Out

▶ what classmates liked about what you shared—and why.

▶ what questions they have.

Chromosphere
CORONA
PHOTOSPHERE
Hydrogen Core
Convective layer
Radiative layer

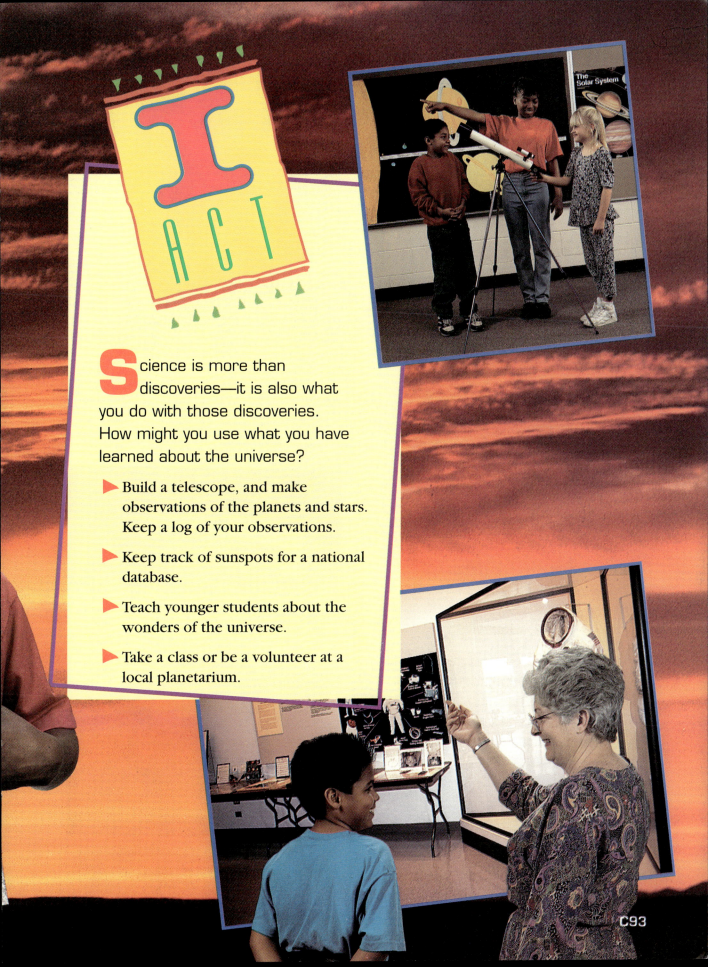

I ACT

Science is more than discoveries—it is also what you do with those discoveries. How might you use what you have learned about the universe?

▶ Build a telescope, and make observations of the planets and stars. Keep a log of your observations.

▶ Keep track of sunspots for a national database.

▶ Teach younger students about the wonders of the universe.

▶ Take a class or be a volunteer at a local planetarium.

THE LANGUAGE OF SCIENCE

The language of science helps people communicate clearly when they talk about the universe. Here are some vocabulary words you can use when you talk about StarBase Earth and the universe with friends, family, and others.

asteroids—small rocky bodies that orbit the sun between the orbits of Mars and Jupiter. **(C45)**

astronomer—a scientist who studies the planets, stars, and other celestial objects in order to understand the universe. **(C15)**

astronomical unit (AU)—the distance between the Earth and the sun, about 150 million kilometers (93 million miles). This unit is used for measuring distances in the solar system. **(C38)**

axis—an imaginary line around which a planet rotates. **(C57)**

▼ Earth's axis is tilted $23\frac{1}{2}°$

Axis

circumpolar—around the poles. Circumpolar stars always appear to circle either the north celestial pole or the south celestial pole. **(C59)**

comets—chunks of ice and rock that travel around the sun in a variety of orbits. Some of the orbits are very long and some are quite short. **(C52)**

▼ Comet

Tail

Head

constellation—a group of stars that appear to make a picture of some sort in the night sky. Ursa Major is a constellation. **(C58)**

▼ Constellation

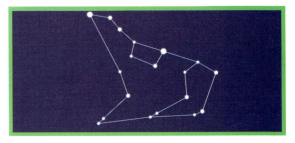

core—the central part of any star. In the core, continual nuclear reactions change hydrogen into helium and energy. **(C76)**

corona—the uppermost gaseous layer of the sun's atmosphere. The corona is visible only during an eclipse. **(C77)**

crater—a deep impression left in the surface of a planet or moon by the impact of a meteorite. **(C34)**

▼ **Crater on the moon**

eclipse—a temporary blocking out of the moon (when the Earth passes between the moon and the sun) or of the sun (when the moon passes between the Earth and the sun). **(C22)**

▼ **Eclipse of the sun**

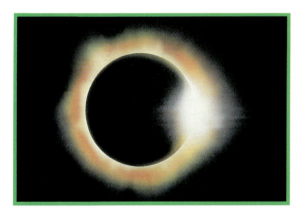

ellipse—a flattened circle, the shape of the orbits of planets and comets. **(C19)**

▼ **Ellipse**

equinox—a day, occurring once in the spring and once in the fall, on which there are equal periods of daylight and night. **(C28)**

galaxy—a vast collection of stars. Our solar system is in the Milky Way galaxy. **(C69)**

gravity/gravitation—the force of attraction between every particle of matter and every other particle of matter. **(C21)**

light-year—the distance light travels in a year, about 10 trillion kilometers (6 trillion miles). **(C71)**

magnitude—the degree of brightness of a star. *Apparent magnitude* is how bright a star appears to observers on Earth. This magnitude is determined by the star's distance from Earth and its actual brightness. *Absolute magnitude* is how bright a star really is. This magnitude is determined by the star's size, color, and mass. **(C81)**

meteor—a meteoroid that enters Earth's atmosphere. When meteors enter Earth's atmosphere, they burn, causing bright flashes of light. **(C53)**

meteorite—a meteor that plunges to Earth in one piece. **(C53)**

▼ **Meteorite impact crater in Arizona**

meteoroid—dust, gas particles, and rocks thrown off by comets. **(C53)**

moon—the Earth's natural satellite. Other planets also have moons. **(C14)**

orbit—the path one object takes around another, such as the path of the Earth around the sun or of the moon around the Earth. **(C16)**

phase—one of the apparent shapes of the moon. The full moon is one phase. **(C30)**

▼ **Phases of the moon**

planet—one of the nine large, solid, nearly spherical objects revolving around the sun. The planets are Mercury, Venus, Earth, Mars, Jupiter, Saturn, Uranus, Neptune, and Pluto. **(C37)**

revolution—the movement of one object around another. One complete revolution of the Earth around the sun takes one Earth year. **(C27)**

rotation—the spinning of a body about its axis. One period of rotation of the Earth takes one Earth day. **(C27)**

satellite—a natural or artificial body that orbits another body. The moon is a natural satellite. **(C43)**

solar system—the sun, its family of planets (including Earth), and all the asteroids, comets, and meteors. **(C37)**

solstice—a day that has the most hours of daylight (summer solstice) or the fewest hours of daylight (winter solstice). **(C28)**

star—a large globe of hot gas, shining by its own light. Different stars go through different stages in their lives. The sun will someday become a *red giant* and then a *white dwarf*. Massive stars may explode into incredibly bright objects called *supernovas*. Then, collapsing in on themselves, they may become *black holes,* from which no light escapes. Some massive stars explode and become very small and dense *neutron stars*. **(C76)**

sun—the star in our solar system. **(C75)**

▼ **Sun's layers**

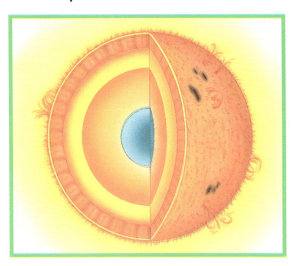

telescope—a device that makes distant objects appear larger, brighter, and more detailed. A *refracting telescope* uses glass lenses to gather light and focus the image. A *reflecting telescope* uses mirrors for the same results. **(C64)**

universe—everything there is—all the planets, solar systems, galaxies, gas, dust, and matter everywhere. **(C73)**

REFERENCE HANDBOOK

Safety in the Classroom

Doing activities in science can be fun, but you need to be sure you do them safely. It is up to you, your teacher, and your classmates to make your classroom a safe place for science activities.

Think about what causes most accidents in everyday life—being careless, not paying attention, and showing off. The same kinds of behavior cause accidents in the science classroom.

Here are some ways to make your classroom a safe place.

THINK AHEAD.
Study the steps of the activity so you know what to expect. If you have any questions about the steps, ask your teacher to explain. Be sure you understand any safety symbols that are shown in the activity.

WATCH YOUR EYES.
Wear safety goggles anytime you are directed to do so. If you should ever get any substance in your eyes, tell your teacher right away.

BE NEAT.
Keep your work area clean. If you have long hair, pull it back so it doesn't get in the way. If you have long sleeves, roll them or push them up to keep them away from your experiment.

OOPS!
If you should have an accident that causes a spill or breaks something, or if you get cut, tell your teacher right away.

YUCK!
Never eat or drink anything during a science activity unless you are told to do so by your teacher.

KEEP IT CLEAN.
Always clean up when you have finished your activity. Put everything away and wipe your work area. Last of all, wash your hands.

DON'T GET SHOCKED.
Sometimes you need to use electric appliances, such as lamps, in an activity. You always need to be careful around electricity. Be sure that electric cords are in a safe place where you can't trip over them. Don't ever pull a plug out of an outlet by pulling on the cord.

Safety Symbols

In some activities, you will see a symbol that stands for what you need to do to stay safe. Do what the symbol stands for.

 This is a general symbol that tells you to be careful. Reading the steps of the activity will tell you exactly what you need to do to be safe.

 You will need to protect your eyes if you see this symbol. Put on safety goggles and leave them on for the entire activity.

 This symbol tells you that you will be using something sharp in the activity. Be careful not to cut or poke yourself or others.

 This symbol tells you something hot will be used in the activity. Be careful not to get burned or to cause someone else to get burned.

 This symbol tells you to put on an apron to protect your clothing.

 Don't touch! This symbol tells you that you will need to touch something that is hot. Use a thermal mitt to protect your hand.

 This symbol tells you that you will be using electric equipment. Use proper safety procedures.

Using a Hand Lens

A hand lens magnifies objects, or makes them look larger than they are.

▲ **This object is not in focus.**

Sometimes objects are too small for you to see easily without some help. You might want to see details that you cannot see with your eyes alone. When this happens, you can use a hand lens.

To use a hand lens, first place the object you want to look at on a flat surface, such as a table. Next, hold the hand lens over the object. At first, the object may appear blurry, like the object in **A**. Move the hand lens toward or away from the object until the object comes into sharp focus, as shown in **B**.

▲ **This object is focused clearly.**

Making a Water-Drop Lens

There may be times when you want to use a hand lens but there isn't one around. If that happens, you can make a water-drop lens to help you in the same way a hand lens does. A water-drop lens is best used to make flat objects, such as pieces of paper and leaves, seem larger.

MATERIALS
- sheet of acetate
- 2 rectangular rubber erasers
- water
- dropper

DO THIS

1 Place the object to be magnified on a table between two identical erasers.

2 Place a sheet of acetate on top of the erasers so that the sheet of acetate is about 1 cm above the object.

3 Use the dropper to place one drop of water on the surface of the sheet over the object. Don't make the drop too large or it will make things look bent.

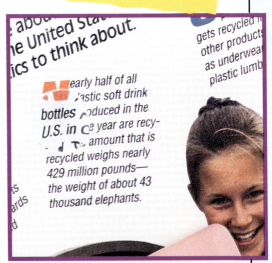

▶ **A water-drop lens can magnify objects.**

Caring For and Using a Microscope

A microscope, like a hand lens, magnifies objects. However, a microscope can increase the detail you see by increasing the number of times an object is magnified.

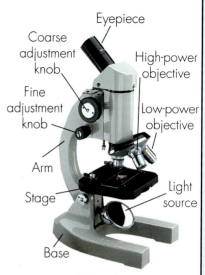

▲ **Light microscope**

CARING FOR A MICROSCOPE

- Always use two hands when you carry a microscope.
- Never touch any of the lenses of the microscope with your fingers.

USING A MICROSCOPE

❶ Raise the eyepiece as far as you can using the coarse-adjustment knob. Place the slide you wish to view on the stage.

❷ Always start by using the lowest power. The lowest-power lens is usually the shortest. Start with the lens in the lowest position it can go without touching the slide.

❸ Look through the eyepiece and begin adjusting the eyepiece upward with the coarse-adjustment knob. When the slide is close to being in focus, use the fine-adjustment knob.

❹ When you want to use the higher-power lens, first focus the slide under low power. Then, watching carefully to make sure that the lens will not hit the slide, turn the higher-power lens into place. Use only the fine-adjustment knob when looking through the higher-power lens.

Some of you may use a Brock microscope. This is a sturdy microscope that has only one lens.

❶ Place the object to be viewed on the stage. Move the long tube, containing the lens, close to the stage.

❷ Put your eye on the eyepiece, and begin raising the tube until the object comes into focus.

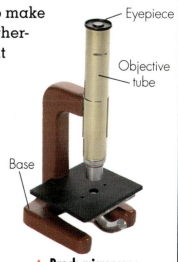

▲ **Brock microscope**

Using a Dropper

Use a dropper when you need to add small amounts of a liquid to another material.

A dropper has two main parts. One is a large empty part called a *bulb*. You hold the bulb and squeeze it to use the dropper. The other part of a dropper is long and narrow and is called a *tube*.

Droppers measure liquids one drop at a time. You might need to figure out how much liquid is in one drop. To do that, you can count the number of drops in 1 mL and divide. For example, if there are about 10 drops in 1 mL, you know that each drop is equal to about 0.1 mL. Follow the directions below to measure a liquid by using a dropper.

DO THIS

❶ Use a clean dropper for each liquid you measure.

❷ With the dropper out of the liquid, squeeze the bulb and keep it squeezed. Then dip the end of the tube into the liquid.

❸ Release the pressure on the bulb. As you do so, you will see the liquid enter the tube.

❹ Take the dropper from the liquid, and move it to the place you want to put the liquid. If you are putting the liquid into another liquid, do not let the dropper touch the surface of the second liquid.

❺ Gently squeeze the bulb until one drop comes out of the tube. Repeat slowly until you have measured out the right number of drops.

▲ **Using a dropper correctly**

▲ **Using a dropper incorrectly**

Measuring Liquids

Use a beaker, a measuring cup, or a graduated cylinder to measure liquids accurately.

Containers for measuring liquids are made of clear or translucent materials so that you can see the liquid inside them. On the outside of each of these measuring tools, you will see lines and numbers that make up a scale. On most of the containers used by scientists, the scale is in milliliters (mL).

DO THIS

1 Pour the liquid you want to measure into one of the measuring containers. Make sure your measuring container is on a flat, stable surface, with the measuring scale facing you.

2 Look at the liquid through the container. Move so that your eyes are even with the surface of the liquid in the container.

3 To read the volume of the liquid, find the scale line that is even with the top of the liquid. In narrow containers, the surface of the liquid may look curved. Take your reading at the lowest point of the curve.

4 Sometimes the surface of the liquid may not be exactly even with a line. In that case, you will need to estimate the volume of the liquid. Decide which line the liquid is closer to, and use that number.

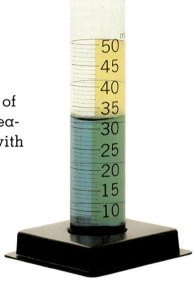

▲ There are 32 mL of liquid in this graduated cylinder.

▲ There are 27 mL of liquid in this beaker.

Using a Thermometer

Determine temperature readings of the air and most liquids by using a thermometer with a standard scale.

Most thermometers are thin tubes of glass that are filled with a red or silver liquid. As the temperature goes up, the liquid in the tube rises. As the temperature goes down, the liquid sinks. The tube is marked with lines and numbers that provide a temperature scale in degrees. Scientists use the Celsius scale to measure temperature. A temperature reading of 27 degrees Celsius is written 27°C.

DO THIS

1 Place the thermometer in the liquid whose temperature you want to record, but don't rest the bulb of the thermometer on the bottom or side of the container. If you are measuring the temperature of the air, make sure that the thermometer is not in direct sunlight or in line with a direct light source.

2 Move so that your eyes are even with the liquid in the thermometer.

3 If you are measuring a material that is not being heated or cooled, wait about two minutes for the reading to become stable. Find the scale line that meets the top of the liquid in the thermometer, and read the temperature.

4 If the material you are measuring is being heated or cooled, you will not be able to wait before taking your measurements. Measure as quickly as you can.

▶ The temperature of this liquid is 27°C.

Making a Thermometer

If you don't have a thermometer, you can make a simple one easily. The simple thermometer won't give you an exact temperature reading, but you can use it to tell if the temperature is going up or going down.

DO THIS

1 Add colored water to the jar until it is nearly full.

2 Place the straw in the jar. Finish filling the jar with water, but leave about 1 cm of space at the top.

3 Lift the straw until 10 cm of it stick up out of the jar. Use the clay to seal the mouth of the jar.

4 Use the dropper to add colored water to the straw until the straw is at least half full.

5 On the straw, mark the level of the water. "S" stands for *start*.

6 To get an idea of how your thermometer works, place the jar in a bowl of ice. Wait several minutes, and then mark the new water level on the straw. This new water level should be marked C for *cold*.

7 Take the jar out of the bowl of ice, and let it return to room temperature. Next, place the jar in a bowl of warm water. Wait several minutes, and then mark the new water level on the straw. This level can be labeled W for *warm*.

MATERIALS

- small, narrow-mouthed jar
- colored water
- clear plastic straw
- ruler
- clay
- dropper
- pen, pencil, or marker
- bowl of ice
- bowl of warm water

W

S

C

▶ You can use a thermometer like this to decide if the temperature of a liquid or the air is going up or down.

Using a Balance

Use a balance to measure an object's mass. Mass is the amount of matter an object has.

Most balances look like the one shown. They have two pans. In one pan, you place the object you want to measure. In the other pan, you place standard masses. Standard masses are objects that have a known mass. Grams are the units used to measure mass for most scientific activities.

DO THIS

1 First, make certain the empty pans are balanced. They are in balance if the pointer is at the middle mark on the base. If the pointer is not at this mark, move the slider to the right or left. Your teacher will help if you cannot balance the pans.

◀ These pans are balanced and ready to be used to find the mass of an object.

2 Place the object you wish to measure in one pan. The pointer will move toward the pan without the object in it.

3 Add the standard masses to the other pan. As you add masses, you should see the pointer begin to move. When the pointer is at the middle mark again, the pans are balanced.

4 Add the numbers on the masses you used. The total is the mass of the object you measured.

▶ These pans are unbalanced.

Making a Balance

If you do not have a balance, you can make one. A balance requires only a few simple materials. You can use nonstandard masses such as paper clips or nickels. This type of balance is best for measuring small masses.

DO THIS

1 If the ruler has holes in it, tie the string through the center hole. If it does not have holes, tie the string around the middle of the ruler.

2 Tape the other end of the string to a table. Allow the ruler to hang down from the side of the table. Adjust the ruler so that it is level.

3 Unbend the end of each paper clip slightly. Push these ends through the paper cups as shown. Attach each cup to the ruler by using the paper clips.

4 Adjust the cups until the ruler is level again.

▶ **This balance is ready for use.**

Using a Spring Scale

A spring scale is a tool you use to measure the force of gravity on objects. You find the weight of the objects and use newtons as the unit of measurement for the force of gravity. You also use the spring scale and newtons to measure other forces.

A spring scale has two main parts. One part is a spring with a hook on the end. The hook is used to connect an object to the spring scale. The other part is a scale with numbers that tell you how many newtons of force are acting on the object.

DO THIS

With an Object at Rest

❶ With the object resting on the table, hook the spring scale to it. Do not stretch the spring at this point.

❷ Lift the scale and object with a smooth motion. Do not jerk them upward.

❸ Wait until any motion in the spring comes to a stop. Then read the number of newtons from the scale.

With an Object in Motion

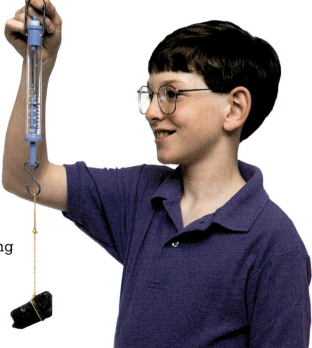

❶ With the object resting on the table, hook the spring scale to it. Do not stretch the spring.

❷ Pull the object smoothly across the table. Do not jerk the object. If you pull with a jerky motion, the spring scale will wiggle too much for you to get a good reading.

❸ As you are pulling, read the number of newtons you are using to pull the object.

Making a Spring Scale

If you do not have a spring scale, you can make one by following the directions below.

DO THIS

1 Staple one end of the rubber band (the part with the sharp curve) to the middle of one end of the cardboard so that the rubber band hangs down the length of the cardboard. Color the loose end of the rubber band with a marker to make it easy to see.

2 Bend the paper clip so that it is slightly open and forms a hook. Hang the paper clip by its unopened end from the rubber band.

3 Put the narrow paper strip across the rubber band, and staple the strip to the cardboard. The rubber band and hook must be able to move easily.

4 While holding the cardboard upright, hang one 100-g mass from the hook. Allow the mass to come to rest, and mark the position of the bottom of the rubber band on the cardboard. Label this position on the cardboard 1 N. Add another 100-g mass for a total of 200 g.

5 Continue to add masses and mark the cardboard. Each 100-g mass adds a force of about 1 N.

MATERIALS
- heavy cardboard (10cm x 30cm)
- large rubber band
- stapler
- marker
- large paper clip
- paper strip (about 1 cm x 3 cm)
- 100-g masses (about 1 N each)

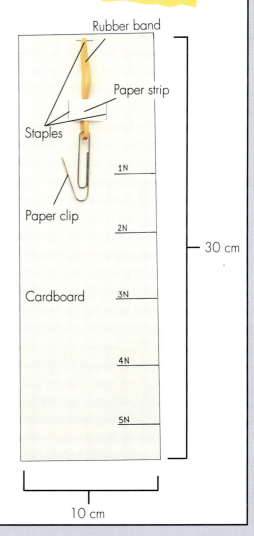

Rubber band
Paper strip
Staples
Paper clip
Cardboard
1N
2N
3N
4N
5N
30 cm
10 cm

Working Like a Scientist

How Clean Is Clean?

In science class, Rachel and Rodney had learned about bacteria and how fast they multiply. They learned that some bacteria are helpful, that most are not harmful to people, and that some can cause diseases.

Rachel and Rodney had learned that disinfectants kill bacteria. They had also found out that there are many different kinds of disinfectants. Each type of disinfectant works a little differently. They wondered, "How can you know which disinfectant will work best for what you want it to do?"

DO THIS

Ask a question.

Form a hypothesis.

Design a test. Do the test.

Record what happened.

Draw a conclusion.

Rachel and Rodney thought about this problem for a while. They put together what they already knew about disinfectants and then came up with a question that they wanted to answer. Rachel and Rodney asked, "Which type of disinfectant kills the most bacteria?"

Often, solving a problem in science starts with reviewing what you already know and *asking a question* about something you want to know. When you review what you already know, you are putting together information and finding out where the gaps are in your knowledge. When you find out what you don't know, you can ask your question. In this case, Rachel and Rodney already knew some things about disinfectants, but they did not know what seemed most important—which disinfectant is most effective.

Rachel and Rodney knew that the next step in their investigation was to suggest an answer to the

question. Rachel asked her father for four kinds of disinfectants. She explained that she wanted to find out how effective they are at killing germs. Her father let her look at the bottles but told her that he would send the disinfectants to the school, where Rachel and Rodney would be working on the investigation. Disinfectants are strong chemicals that must be handled with caution.

Rachel looked at the labels on the bottles, but they all said similar kinds of things. One label claimed, "Kills any germ it touches." The ingredients in all of the bottles were different, and Rachel couldn't even read the names of most of them. She knew she couldn't figure out how each chemical worked.

Because Rachel did not know how the chemicals worked, she did not know which one would be most effective. She didn't see any reason why they all wouldn't work equally well. Rachel's suggested answer, or hypothesis, to her question was that all of the disinfectants would work equally well to kill bacteria.

The next day at school, Rachel shared her information with Rodney. He agreed with her reasoning, and they decided to use the four disinfectants Rachel's father had sent in.

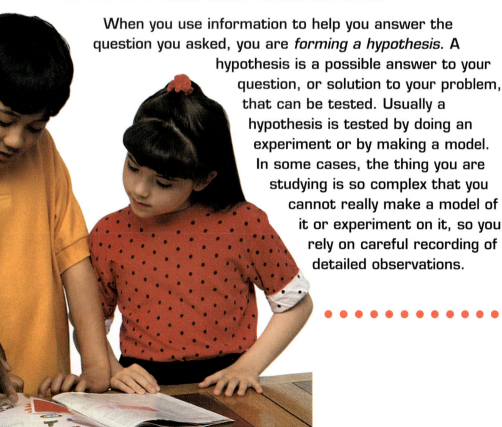

DO THIS

Ask a question.

Form a hypothesis.

Design a test. Do the test.

Record what happened.

Draw a conclusion.

When you use information to help you answer the question you asked, you are *forming a hypothesis.* A hypothesis is a possible answer to your question, or solution to your problem, that can be tested. Usually a hypothesis is tested by doing an experiment or by making a model. In some cases, the thing you are studying is so complex that you cannot really make a model of it or experiment on it, so you rely on careful recording of detailed observations.

After you have asked a question and formed a hypothesis, you must somehow test the hypothesis. One of the most common types of test is an *experiment.* It is important to remember that a single experiment does not prove that a hypothesis is right. However, a single experiment may be enough to show that a hypothesis is not right and needs to be changed. The most important thing to remember when you are designing an experiment is that it must be focused on the question. For example, it is not useful to do an experiment that measures the pollutants in the air each day if you want to know how air pressure affects rainfall.

Rachel and Rodney worked with their teacher, Mr. Gormand, to design an experiment. They decided to grow bacteria in five dishes. Four of the dishes would be treated with different disinfectants. One of the dishes would be untreated.

Rachel and Rodney knew that it was important in any good experiment to have a control. A *control* is a sample or setup in which you don't change any variables. So the dish that was not treated with a disinfectant was their control. For any good experiment, you compare the results from your control to the results from your other samples to see if there is any difference. If there is no difference between the control and a sample, then the treatment you gave the sample had no effect.

Mr. Gormand showed Rachel and Rodney five dishes containing a substance that looked like beige gelatin. Mr. Gormand explained that the gelatinlike material was food for bacteria. He also explained that bacteria were added to the food substance before it was poured into the dishes. Then Mr. Gormand showed them four small disks made of absorbent paper. Each disk was soaked in a different disinfectant. Mr. Gormand placed a treated disk in each of four dishes. In the fifth dish, the control, Mr. Gormand placed an untreated paper disk. Mr. Gormand told Rachel and Rodney what to look for in each dish. As the bacteria multiply, they form colonies that are visible as little dots. As the bacteria increase in number, the colonies grow larger. Mr. Gormand told Rachel and Rodney that if a disinfectant killed the bacteria, a clear area— no colonies—would be found around the disk. The larger the clear area, the more effective the disinfectant. Each day, Rachel and Rodney would measure the width of the clear area from the edge of the dish to where the bacterial colonies started. They would measure the clear areas every day for five days.

Because it is very dangerous to work with live bacteria, Mr. Gormand did all of the treatments. He allowed Rachel and Rodney to handle the dishes only after the dishes were sealed, and he instructed them to wash their hands very carefully after recording their information for the day.

When you do an experiment, you must collect information. Another word for the information you collect is *data.* When you collect data, you are *recording your observations* and the results of your experiment so that someone else can understand what happened. You must not only record the information but also organize it. Organization is important if you want people to understand what you have discovered. There are many different ways to organize data. Two of the more common ways are making tables and making graphs.

DO THIS

| Ask a question. |
| Form a hypothesis. |
| Design a test. Do the test. |
| Record what happened. |
| Draw a conclusion. |

Each day, Rachel and Rodney measured the clear area around each treated paper disk. They also observed the disk that was left untreated. Why did they need to look at the untreated disk? They recorded their measurements in a table each day. They then used the information in their table to make a line graph.

Often, information in a table is hard to read and understand. A graph is a good summary for many types of data.

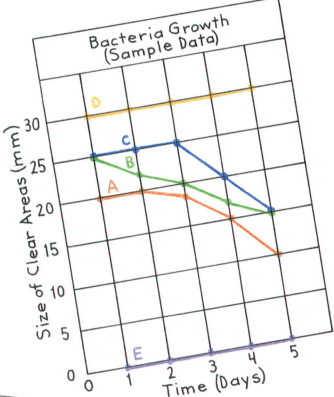

Growth of Bacteria (Sample Data)
Size of Clear Areas (mm)

	A	B	C	D	E (Control)
Day 1	20	25	25	30	0
Day 2	20	22	25	30	0
Day 3	19	20	25	30	0
Day 4	15	17	21	30	0
Day 5	10	15	15	30	0

Once all of your information is collected, you must use that information to *draw a conclusion.* One thing you are looking for when you draw a conclusion is to see if your hypothesis is supported. If your hypothesis is not supported by the results of the experiment, then it is most likely incorrect.

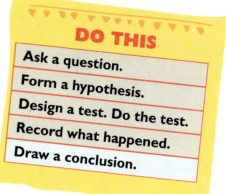

DO THIS

Ask a question.

Form a hypothesis.

Design a test. Do the test.

Record what happened.

Draw a conclusion.

Remember, an incorrect hypothesis is not a failure! Not at all. An incorrect hypothesis helps you eliminate one possible answer to a question. You can then design experiments to focus on other possible answers. Also remember that if the experiment does support your hypothesis, that does not mean your hypothesis is proven. You may have to change your hypothesis a little as a result of your experiment.

You've already seen Rachel and Rodney's data. Look back at their hypothesis. Was their hypothesis supported by the data?

Rachel and Rodney concluded that their hypothesis was not supported. What they saw in the experiment clearly showed that some disinfectants worked far better than others. They concluded that the reason some disinfectants were better was that the chemicals in the disinfectants were different.

Rachel and Rodney still did not know how the chemicals killed the bacteria. And because each bottle had many different kinds of chemicals, they did not even know which of the chemicals was the disinfectant.

Rachel and Rodney concluded that they knew that disinfectants differed in their ability to control bacteria, but they did not know why this was so. Rachel suggested that they might continue their experiments by testing two very similar disinfectants. They could compare the actions of the two mixtures and then decide what contributed most to the disinfectant.

Often conclusions in experiments will raise other questions for which you might want to find answers. The solutions to problems often raise new problems to solve. This is one way in which progress is made in science.

INDEX

Note: Page numbers in italics indicate illustrations.

ACKNOWLEDGMENTS

For permission to reprint copyrighted material, grateful acknowledgment is made to the following sources:

Career World® Magazine: "So, You Wanna Be a Chef? Be Prepared . . . to Train Like an Athlete" by Joanne Koch from *Career World®* Magazine, May 1992. Text copyright © 1992 by Weekly Reader Corporation. Published by Weekly Reader Corporation.

Carolrhoda Books, Inc., Minneapolis, MN: Cover photograph by Cheryl Walsh Bellville from *American Bison* by Ruth Berman. Photograph copyright © 1992 by Cheryl Walsh Bellville. Cover illustration by Peter J. Thornton from *Everybody Cooks Rice* by Norah Dooley. Copyright © 1991 by Carolrhoda Books, Inc.

Children's Television Workshop, New York, NY: "The Inside Story: A Fantastic Voyage Through the Human Body" by Beth Chayet from *3-2-1 Contact* Magazine, June 1992. Text copyright 1992 by Children's Television Workshop. "Incredible Edibles: Unusual Food from Around the World" by Elizabeth Keyishian from *3-2-1 Contact* Magazine, June 1989. Text copyright 1989 by Children's Television Workshop. "Do Me a Flavor! Scientists Cook Up New Tastes" by Eric Weiner from *3-2-1 Contact* Magazine, May 1989. Text copyright 1989 by Children's Television Workshop.

Clarion Books, a Houghton Mifflin Company imprint: Cover illustration by Alix Berenzy from *The Princess in the Pigpen* by Jane Resh Thomas. Illustration © 1989 by Alix Berenzy.

Crown Publishers, Inc.: Cover photograph from *Voyager: An Adventure to the Edge of the Solar System* by Sally Ride and Tam O'Shaughnessy. Photograph © 1991 by Roger Ressmeyer/Starlight.

Current Health 1® Magazine: "Food Additives: A Closer Look at Labels" from *Current Health 1®* Magazine, February 1989. Text copyright © 1989 by Weekly Reader Corporation. "Preserving the Prairie—A Return to Tallgrass" from *Current Health 1®* Magazine, December 1993. Text copyright © 1993 by Weekly Reader Corporation. From "Stop That Germ!" in *Current Health 1®* Magazine, October 1993. Text copyright © 1993 by Weekly Reader Corporation. *Current Health 1®* Magazine is published by Weekly Reader Corporation.

Delacorte Press, a division of Bantam Doubleday Dell Publishing Group, Inc.: Cover illustration by Neal McPheeters from *Wings: The Last Book of the Bromeliad* by Terry Pratchett. Illustration copyright © 1991 by Neal McPheeters.

Dorling Kindersley, Inc.: Cover illustration from *Weather* by John Farndon. Copyright © 1992 by Dorling Kindersley Ltd., London.

Aileen Fisher: "Clouds" by Aileen Fisher from *In the Woods, in the Meadow, in the Sky.* Text copyright © 1965 by Scribner's, New York.

David R. Godine, Publisher, Inc.: Cover illustration by Jonathan Allen from *Burton & Stanley* by Frank O'Rourke. Illustration copyright © 1993 by Jonathan Allen.

Greenwillow Books, a division of William Morrow & Company, Inc.: "No, I Won't Turn Orange" from *The New Kid on the Block* by Jack Prelutsky. Text copyright © 1984 by Jack Prelutsky.

Peggy Guthart: "Ready for Spaghetti" by Peggy Guthart. Text copyright 1991 by Peggy Guthart.

Holt, Rinehart and Winston, Inc.: From "David Powless, Conservationist" in *Holt Life Science.* Text copyright © 1994 by Holt, Rinehart and Winston, Inc.

Dean Kennedy: Cover illustration by Dean Kennedy from *Burton's Zoom Zoom Va-ROOM Machine* by Dorothy Haas. Illustration copyright © 1990 by Dean Kennedy.

Alfred A. Knopf, Inc.: "January" from *A Child's Calendar* by John Updike. Text copyright © 1965 by John Updike; text copyright renewed 1993 by John Updike.

Lodestar Books, an affiliate of Dutton Children's Books, a division of Penguin Books USA Inc.: Cover illustration by Ted Enik from *Why Can't You Unscramble an Egg?* by Vicki Cobb. Illustration copyright © 1990 by Ted Enik.

The Millbrook Press: Cover illustration by Sal Murdocca from *EUREKA! It's an Automobile!* by Jeanne Bendick. Illustration copyright © 1992 by Sal Murdocca.

National Geographic WORLD: "The Great Flood of 1993" by Barbara Brownell from *National Geographic WORLD* Magazine, October 1993. Text copyright 1993 by National Geographic Society. "Surviving Andrew, 1992's Biggest Hurricane!" by Judith E. Rinard from *National Geographic WORLD* Magazine, April 1993. Text copyright 1993 by National Geographic Society. From "Seeing Stars" by Judith E. Rinard in *National Geographic WORLD* Magazine, July 1993. Text copyright 1993 by National Geographic Society. "Chute for the (Sports) Stars" from *National Geographic WORLD* Magazine, July 1993. Text copyright 1993 by National Geographic Society.

National Wildlife Federation: "I Spy on Prairie Dogs" by Mark Hoogland, as told to Gary Turbak from *Ranger Rick* Magazine, September 1988. Text copyright 1988 by the National Wildlife Federation. "Lightning" by Robert Irby from *Ranger Rick* Magazine, August 1983. Text copyright 1983 by the National Wildlife Federation.

William Noonan: Cover illustration by William Noonan from *The Place of Lions* by Eric Campbell. Copyright © 1991, 1990 by Eric Campbell. Published by Harcourt Brace & Company.

Scholastic Inc.: "Cell Theory Rap" by Deborah Carver from *SCIENCE WORLD,* October 1990. Text copyright © 1990 by Scholastic Inc.

Steck-Vaughn Company: Cover design from *Facing the Future: Choosing Health* by Alan Collinson.

University of Nebraska Press: From p. 95 in *Dust Bowl Diary* by Ann Marie Low. Text copyright 1984 by the University of Nebraska Press.

Franklin Watts, Inc., New York: From *Lyme Disease* (Retitled: "The Puzzle") by Elaine Landau. Text copyright © 1990 by Elaine Landau.

PHOTOGRAPHY CREDITS:

KEY: (t)top, (b)bottom, (l)left, (r)right, (c)center, (bg)background

FRONT COVER, Harcourt Brace & Co. Photographs: (tl), (tr), (b), Greg Leary.
All Other Photographs: (c), Terje Rakke/The Image Bank; (cr), Ewing Galloway.
BACK COVER, (tl), Biophoto Assoc./Science Source/Photo Researchers; (tr), Phil Degginger/Bruce Coleman, Inc.; (b), Antony Miles/Bruce Coleman, Inc.
TABLE OF CONTENTS, Harcourt Brace & Co. Photographs: Page:iv(br), v(tl), Terry D. Sinclair; vii(tr), Weronica Ankarorn; vii(br), Terry D. Sinclair; viii(b), Terry D. Sinclair; ix(tl), Weronica Ankarorn.
All Other Photographs: Page: iv(tl), Photri; iv(tr), Runk/Schoenberger/Grant Heilman; iv(bl), Peter Menzel; v(tr), David A. Wagner/PHOTOTAKE; v(bl), NIBSC/SPL/Photo Researchers; v(br), Peter Menzel; vi(tl), Roger Ressmeyer/Starlight; vi(tr), Giraudon/Art Resource; vi(b), NASA/JSC/Starlight; vii(tl), David R. Frazier Photolibrary; vii(bl), First Light; viii(tl), L.L. Rue, Jr./Bruce Coleman, Inc.; viii(c), Amy Etra/PhotoEdit; viii-ix(b), Lefever/Grushow/Grant Heilman Photography; ix(tr), Ann Purcell/Photo Researchers; ix(br), Mike Khansa/The Image Bank.
TO THE STUDENT: Harcourt Brace & Company Photographs: Page:xi(b), xiii, xvi(l), Terry D. Sinclair.
All Other Photographs: Page: x(b), xi(t), David Young-Wolff/PhotoEdit; xii, The Stock Market; xiv(l), Bob Daemmrich Photography; xiv(r), Myrleen Ferguson/PhotoEdit; xv(t), David Young-Wolff/PhotoEdit; xv(b), Comstock; xvi(r), David Young-Wolff/PhotoEdit.
UNIT A: Harcourt Brace & Company Photographs: Page: A4-A5, A6(t), A6(c), A6(b), Terry D. Sinclair; A8, A9, Weronica Ankarorn; A10-A11, Terry D. Sinclair; A14, Weronica Ankarorn; A15, A18, A20(t), A20(b), A21, A28, Terry D. Sinclair; A29(t), Weronica Ankarorn; A36, A38, A39, A40, A41, A42, A44-A45, Terry D. Sinclair; A44, Maria Paraskevas; A47, A49, A53, A54, A55, A60, A63, A66-A67, A73(bg), A73, Terry D. Sinclair; A75, Weronica Ankarorn; A77(t), A77(b), A82, A84, A90-A91(inset), A91(tr), A92(t), A92(b), Terry D. Sinclair; A93(t), Weronica Ankarorn.
All Other Photographs: Page: Divider Page A, Peter Menzel; A1, A2-A3, Tony Freeman/PhotoEdit; A3(inset), F.K. Smith; A7, Mike Morris/Unicorn Stock Photos; A12(border), Joyce Photographics/Photo Researchers; A12, Johnny Autery; A12(inset), M. Antman/The Image Works; A13, Jan Halaska/Photo Researchers; A14(inset), Bill Horsman/Stock, Boston; A16(t), M. Antman/The Image Works; A16(c), John Elk III/Stock, Boston; A16(bl), Jeff Greenberg/Unicorn Stock Photos; A16(r), Courtesy Thermometer Corp. of America/Color-Pic; A17(tl), David R. Frazier/The Stock Solution; A17(tr), The Granger Collection, New York; A17(b), Tom Pantages; A20-A21(bg), Craig Tuttle/The Stock Market; A23, Kent & Donna Dannen/Photo Researchers; A23 (inset), Bob Daemmrich/The Image Works; A25, Charles Krebs/The Stock Market; A26, E.R. Degginger/Color-Pic; A29(ct), Myrleen Ferguson Cate/PhotoEdit; A29(cb), Bob Daemmrich/Stock, Boston; A29(b), Kees Van Den Berg/Photo Researchers; A30, Myrleen Ferguson Cate/PhotoEdit; A30(inset), Richard Pasley/Stock, Boston; A31(l), Joyce Photographics/Photo Researchers; A31(r), E.R. Degginger/Color Pic; A32-A33, J.A. Borowczyk/The Stock Solution; A33, Tom McCarthy/Unicorn Stock Photos; A34(t), Lee Rentz/Bruce Coleman, Inc.; A34(c), A34(b), E.R. Degginger/Color-Pic; A35(tl), Nancy L. Simmerman/Bruce Coleman, Inc.; A35(tr), E.R. Degginger/Color-Pic; A35(b), Phil Degginger/Color-Pic; A42-A43(bg), E.R. Degginger/Color-Pic; A42-A43(inset), Tony Freeman/PhotoEdit; A46(border), Dan Sudia/Photo Researchers; A46, Timothy Schultz/Bruce Coleman, Inc.; A46(inset), Photri; A48, Phil Degginger/Color-Pic; A49(bg), H. Bluestein/Photo Researchers; A50-A51, Peter Menzel; A54-A55(bg), Tony Freeman/PhotoEdit; A56-A57, Nawrocki Stock Photo; A57, Ralf-Finn Hestoft/SABA; A58-A59, Susan Poa/Times Picayune/AP/Wide World Photos; A59(t), Howard B. Bluestein/Photo Researchers; A60(bg), E.R. Degginger/Color-Pic; A61(all), Howard B.

Bluestein/Photo Researchers; A62, University of Southern Indiana Special Collections; A64, Edward Slater/Southern Stock Photo Agency; A65, Raymond K. Gehman; A67(t), Lynne Sladky/AP/Wide World Photos; A69(t), Gaston DeCardenas/AP/Wide World Photos; A69(b) Vince Streano/Tony Stone Images; A71, John M. Discher/AP/Wide World Photos; A72(border), E.R. Degginger/Color-Pic; A72, John Shaw/Bruce Coleman, Inc.; A72(inset), Peter Southwick/Stock, Boston; A74-A75, Dan Sudia/Photo Researchers; A74, Chris Sorensen; A76(l), Rod Planck/Photo Researchers; A76(c), Thomas R. Fletcher/Stock, Boston; A76(r), Dr. Eckart Pott/Bruce Coleman, Inc.; A79, Kunio Owaki/The Stock Market; A80, Tom Brakefield/Bruce Coleman, Inc.; A81, A82(bg), The Bettmann Archive; A83(l), Tony Freeman/PhotoEdit; A83(r), Randall Hyman/Stock, Boston; A86(t), Robert Caputo/Stock, Boston; A86(c), Carl Frank/Photo Researchers; A86(b), James A. Sugar/Black Star; A87(t), Robert Caputo/Stock, Boston; A87(c), A87(b), James A. Sugar/Black Star; A90-A91(bg), A. & J. Verkaik/The Stock Market; A91(tl), Van Bucher/Photo Researchers; A92-A93(bg), Kees Van Den Berg/Photo Researchers; A93(b), Mary Kate Denny/PhotoEdit; A94(t), Lee Rentz/Bruce Coleman, Inc.; A94(c), E.R. Degginger/Color-Pic; A94(b), Phil Degginger/Color-Pic.

UNIT B: Harcourt Brace & Company Photographs: Page: B4-B5, B6(c), B7(t), B7(c), B7(b), Terry D. Sinclair; B8, B9, Weronica Ankarorn; B10-B11, B12 (inset), Terry D. Sinclair; B13, Charlie Burton; B19, B20, B21, B22(all), B23, B26, B28, B37, B40, B41, B49, B50, B51, B52, B53, B54, B59, B70, B73, B74-B75, B75(tl), B76(t), B76(b), Terry D. Sinclair; B77(t), Weronica Ankarorn; B77(b), Terry D. Sinclair; B79(c), Terry D. Sinclair; B79(b), Weronica Ankarorn.

All Other Photographs: Page: Divider Page B, Professors P.M. Motta & T. Fujita/SPL/Photo Researchers; B1, B2-B3, Bob Gossington/Bruce Coleman, Inc.; B3 (inset), NIBSC/SPL; B6(t), Franken/Stock, Boston; B6(b), Bob Daemmrich/Stock, Boston; B12 (border), Ed Reschke/Peter Arnold, Inc.; B12, Michael Abbey/Photo Researchers; B14(t), Stepanowicz/Bruce Coleman, Inc.; B14(b), The Granger Collection, New York; B15(t), H. Reinhard/Bruce Coleman, Inc.; B15(ct), E.R. Degginger/Photo Researchers; B15(c), David Scharf/Peter Arnold, Inc.; B15(cb), David Madison/Bruce Coleman, Inc.; B15(b), Farrell Grehan/Photo Researchers; B16(b), Peter Menzel; B16-B17, Biophoto Associates/Science Source/Photo Researchers; B18(t),Runk/Schoenberger/ Grant Heilman Photography; B18(b), Barry L. Runk/Grant Heilman Photography; B24(all), M. Abbey/Photo Researchers; B25(t), Petit Format/ Nestle/Science Source/Photo Researchers; B25(ct), C.J. Allen/Stock, Boston; B25(cb), Richard Hutchings/Photo Researchers; B25(b), David Madison/Bruce Coleman, Inc.; B28 (border), E.R. Degginger/Bruce Coleman, Inc.; B28 (inset), M Abbey/Photo Researchers; B29, Biology Media/Photo Researchers; B30(t), Biomedical Communications/Bruce Coleman, Inc.; B30(c), Biophoto Associates/Science Source/Photo Researchers; B30(b), E.R. Degginger/Bruce Coleman, Inc.; B31(t), Ed Reschke/Peter Arnold, Inc.; B31(c), Ed Reschke/Peter Arnold, Inc.; B31(b), David A. Wagner/PHOTOTAKE; B32(t), M. Abbey/Photo Researchers; B32(c), M. Abbey/Photo Researchers; B32(b), Martin Rotker/PHO-TOTAKE; B34, B35(t), B35(c), B36(t), B36(b), Lennart Nilsson, THE INCREDIBLE MACHINE, National Geographic Society; B38, Bruce Iverson/SPL/Photo Researchers; B39(t), Professors P.M. Motta & T. Fujita/SPL/Photo Researchers; B39(c), CNRI/SPL/Photo Researchers; B39(b), Manfred Kage/Peter Arnold, Inc.; B43, Peter Menzel; B50(border), CDC/Peter Arnold, Inc.; B50 (inset), NCI/Science Source/Photo Researchers; B55, David Wagner/PHOTOTAKE; B56(t), David M. Phillips/Photo Researchers; 56(b), M.I. Walker/Photo Researchers; B57(t), Manfred Kage/Peter Arnold, Inc.; B57(bl), Omikron/Science Source/Photo Researchers; B57(bcl), Dr. Tony Brain/SPL/Photo Researchers; B57(bcr), David Phillips/Photo Researchers; B57(br), Manfred Kage/Peter Arnold, Inc.; B58(l), A.B. Dowsett/SPL/Photo Researchers; B58(c), Omikron/Science Source/Photo Researchers; B58(r), A.B. Dowsett/SPL/Photo Researchers; B61, Chuck Savage/The Stock Market; B62(t), Thomas Fletcher/Stock, Boston; B62(c), M.I. Walker/Science Source/Photo Researchers; B62(b), M. Abbey/Photo Researchers; B63(t), Alfred Pasieka/Peter Arnold, Inc.; B63(ct), C.C. Duncan/Medical Images; B63(c), Manfred Kage/Peter Arnold, Inc.; B63(cb), Martin Dohrn/Photo Researchers; B63(b), E. Gueho-CNRI/SPL/Photo Researchers; B64, Scott Camazine/Photo Researchers; B65, Kent Wood/Peter Arnold, Inc.; B66, Prof. P. Motta/Dept. of Anatomy/Univ. of "La Sapienza", Rome/SPL/Photo Researchers; B67(t), Biophoto Associates/Photo Researchers; B67(b), B68, Peter Menzel; B69, The Granger Collection, New York; B71, The Bettmann Archive; B72(t), B72(b), HRW Photo; B74-B75(bg), Omikron/Science Source/Photo Researchers; B75(tr), Manfred Kage/Peter Arnold, Inc.; B79(t), C.C. Duncan/Medical Images.

UNIT C: Harcourt Brace & Company Photographs: Page: C4-C5, C6(c), C6(b), Terry D. Sinclair; C7(t inset), Maria Paraskevas; C7(b), Terry D. Sinclair; C8, C9, Weronica Ankarorn; C10-C11, C13, C14, C17(t), C17(b), C19, C21(t), C22, C27, C37(b), C40, Terry D. Sinclair; C50, Weronica Ankarorn; C55, Terry D. Sinclair; C58, Weronica Ankarorn; C60, C65, C66, C70, C78, C80, C85(tl), C90-C91, C91(tl), C91(tr), C92(t), C92(b), C93(t), Terry D. Sinclair.

All Other Photographs: Page: Divider Page C, NASA; C1, C2-C3, Dr. Jean Lorre/SPL/Photo Researchers; C3, JPL/NASA; C6 (t), J. Hester/Arizona State University/NASA; C7(t), Photo by P. Hollembeak, Courtesy Department of Library Services, American Museum of Natural History; C12 (border), Comstock; C12, NASA; C12(inset), Luis Vilotta/The Stock Market; C14(bg), NASA/JSC/Starlight; C15(l), Art Resource; C15(r), Ron Watts/First Light; C16,

Archiv fur Kunst und Geschichte; C18(t), NASA/JSC/ Starlight; C18(b), NASA, C19(bg), NASA; C20(bg), Michael Freeman; C20, Bridgeman Art Library/Art Resource, NY; C22(bg), Dennis DiCiccio/Peter Arnold, Inc.; C22(b), Roger Ressmeyer/Starlight; C23(t), Dennis DiCiccio/Peter Arnold, Inc.; C23(b), Roger Ressmeyer/Starlight; C24-C25, G. Petersen/First Light; C25(tl), Mary Evans Picture Library; C25(tr), M. Timothy O'Keefe/Tom Stack & Associates; C25(c), Jack Parsons; C25(b), Giraudon/Art Resource, NY; C26-C27(bg), Comstock; C29(t), Thomas Kitchin/Tom Stack & Associates; C29(b) Thomas Kitchin/Tom Stack & Associates; C30(all) The Observatories of the Carnegie Institution of Washington; C32, NASA; C33(l), Michael Mendillo/Boston University, Center for Space Physics; C33(r), NASA; C34(t), The Observatories of the Carnegie Institution of Washington; C34-C35, NASA; C35(tl), NASA; C35(tr), Hale Observatories, Polomar Mountain California; C36, JPL/NASA; C36(inset), JPL/NASA; C36(border), NASA; C37(t), U.S.G.S. Flagstaff Arizona/Starlight; C41(t), JPL/NASA; C41(c), Edmond Scientific Company/NASA; C41(b), U.S.G.S./Starlight; C42, NASA/JSC Starlight; C43, NASA; C44(c), NASA/JPL; C44(r), NASA; C44(c), NASA/JPL; C44(bg), U.S.S.R. Flagstaff Arizona/Starlight; C45(t), JPL/NASA; C45(b), NASA; C46(all photos) JPL/NASA; C47(bg), NASA; C47, Peter Arnold, Inc.; C48(t), STSI/NASA; C48(b), NASA; C49(t), The Bettman Archive; C49(b), Michael Freeman; C51(t), JPL/NASA; C51(c), JPL/NASA; C51(b), STSI/NASA; C53, Dennis Milon; C54, The Arecibo Observatory is part of the National Astronomy and Ionosphere Center which is operated by Cornell University under a cooperative agreement with the National Science Foundation; C56(border), Roger Ressmeyer/Starlight; C56, Courtesy/Royal Observatory Edinburgh, Photographed by David Malin; C56(inset), Vaughn/Tom Stack & Associates; C62-C63(all photos), Ian Howarth; C64(l), Scala/Art Resource; C64(r), The Bettman Archive; C67(b), Ressmeyer/Starlight; C67(all other photos), Roger Ressmeyer/Starlight; C68(t), NASA/The Image Works; C68(bl), STSI/NASA; C68(br), STSI/NASA; C69, Frank Rossotto/Tom Stack & Associates; C72(tl), Courtesy/Anglo Australian Observatory, Photographed by David Malin; C72(r), Palomar Observatory; C72(bl), JPL; C73, Courtesy/Anglo Australian Observatory, Photographed by David Malin; C74(border), First Light; C74, Kim Gordon/SPL/Photo Researchers; C74(inset), Roger Ressmeyer/Starlight; NASA; C75(tr), Stocktrek Photo Agency/SPL/Tom Stack & Assoc.; C75(bl), Frank Rossotto/Tom Stack & Assoc.; C75(br), NASA/JPL; C81, John Sandford/SPL/Photo Researchers; C83, Geoff Williams & Howard Metcalf/SPL/Photo Researchers; C84(tl), Hank Morgan/Rainbow; C84(tlc), David R. Frazier Photolibrary; C84(trc), M. Siluk/The Image Works; C84(tr), William H. Edwards/The Image Bank; C84(bl), NASA; C84(blc), J. Heap/Goddard Space Flight Center/NASA; C84(brc), Courtesy/Royal Observatory Edinburgh, Photographed by David Malin; C84(br), NRAO/AUI/SPL/Photo Researchers; C85(tlc), First Light; C85(trc), Steve Krongard/The Image Bank; C85(tr), Kapteryn Laboratorium/SPL/Photo Researchers; C85(bl), JPL; C85(br), Ray Nelson/Phototake; C86, Roger Ressmeyer/Starlight; C90-C91(bg), STSI/NASA; C91(c), Walzenbach/The Stock Market; C92-C93(bg), Craig Aurness/First Light; C93(bg,b), Bob Abraham/The Stock Market; C94, W. Hille/Leo de Wys, Inc.; C95(tl), Hansen Planetarium/NASA Photo; C95(r), Barrie Rokeach/The Image Bank; C95(bl), Roger Ressmeyer/Starlight; C96(all), The Observatories of the Carnegie Institution of Washington.

UNIT D: Harcourt Brace & Company Photographs: Page: D4-D5, D6(t), D6(c), D6(b), D7(c), Terry D. Sinclair; D7(b), Greg Leary; D8, Weronica Ankarorn; D9, Maria Paraskevas; D10-D11, Terry D. Sinclair; D12(bg), Weronica Ankarorn; D13, Maria Paraskevas; D15(t), Terry D. Sinclair; D16(t), Weronica Ankarorn; D19, D20(bg), D20, D21, Terry D. Sinclair; D24(t), Weronica Ankarorn; D24(b), D25(t), Maria Paraskevas; D25(c), Terry D. Sinclair; D25(b), Maria Paraskevas; D27, D28(b), Terry D. Sinclair; D29, Maria Paraskevas; D30(bl), D31, Terry D. Sinclair; D32, Maria Paraskevas; D33, Terry D. Sinclair; D34(tl), D34(tc), D34(bl), Weronica Ankarorn; D34(br), Terry D. Sinclair; D36 (border), D36, D36 (inset), D37, Weronica Ankarorn; D38, Maria Paraskevas; D39, Terry D. Sinclair; D41, D42(t), D42(b), Weronica Ankarorn; D43(bg), D43(inset), D44(t), Terry D. Sinclair; D44(b), Maria Paraskevas; D45, D46, D47, D48 (bg), D48, Terry D. Sinclair; D49, Weronica Ankarorn; D50, Terry D. Sinclair; D51(br), Weronica Ankarorn; D52, D57, Terry D. Sinclair; D58, Maria Paraskevas; D62, Terry D. Sinclair; D63, Maria Paraskevas; D64, Terry D. Sinclair; D66 (border), Maria Paraskevas; D67, D68-D69(bg), D68, D69, D70(t), Terry D. Sinclair; D70(b), Weronica Ankarorn; D72(t), D77, D79, D81, D88(c), D89, D90-D91(bg), D90-D91(tr), Terry D. Sinclair; D90(bl), Weronica Ankarorn; D91, Terry D. Sinclair; D92-D93(b), D93(t), D93(b), D94(b), D95(tl), Terry D. Sinclair; D95(tcr), D95(tr), Maria Paraskevas; D95(b all), Terry D. Sinclair.

All Other Photographs: Page: Divider Page D, First Light; D1, D2-D3, Michael Skott; D3, Richard Embery/FPG; D7(t), Brian King/Leo de Wys, Inc.; D12, Dan Lecca/FPG; D12(inset), David R. FrazierPhotolibrary; D14, Courtesy of International Flavors & Fragrances, John Olson, photographer; D16(b), Thomas Kitchin/First Light; D17-D18, Courtesy of International Flavors & Fragrances, John Olson, photographer; D23, Alexander Marshack; D28(l), NASA; D28(tr), John Bova/ Photo Researchers; D30(bg), Tony Freeman/PhotoEdit; D34(tr), Terje Rakke/The Image Bank; D35, Rod Planck/Photo Researchers; D40, Steve Short/First Light; D51(t), Robert Brenner/PhotoEdit; D51(bl), Yoav Levy/PHOTOTAKE; D51(bc), Yoav Levy/PHO-TOTAKE; D53, Leo de Wys, Inc.; D54(t), NASA; D54(b), Photographed by Ted